SUPER EASY SONGBOOK

CHRISTMAS SONGS

D1592304

ISBN 978-1-4950-9705-8

HAL•LEONARD®

7777 W. BLUEMOUND RD. P.O. BOX 13819 MILWAUKEE, WI 53213

Visit Hal Leonard Online at
www.halleonard.com

Welcome to the *Super Easy Songbook* series!

This unique collection will help you play your favorite songs quickly and easily. Here's how it works:

- Play the simplified melody with your right hand. Letter names appear inside each note to assist you.

- There are no key signatures to worry about! If a sharp ♯ or flat ♭ is needed, it is shown beside the note each time.

- There are no page turns, so your hands never have to leave the keyboard.

- If two notes are connected by a tie ⌣, hold the first note for the combined number of beats. (The second note does not show a letter name since it is not re-struck.)

- Add basic chords with your left hand using the provided keyboard diagrams. Chord voicings have been carefully chosen to minimize hand movement.

- The left-hand rhythm is up to you, and chord notes can be played together or separately. Be creative!

- If the chords sound muddy, move your left hand an octave* higher. If this gets in the way of playing the melody, move your right hand an octave higher as well.

  * An octave spans eight notes. If your starting note is C, the next C to the right is an octave higher.

--------------------------- ALSO AVAILABLE ---------------------------

Hal Leonard Student Keyboard Guide HL00296039

Key Stickers HL00100016

All I Want for Christmas Is My Two Front Teeth

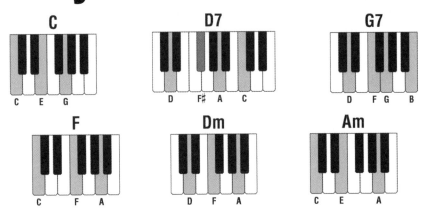

Words and Music by
Don Gardner

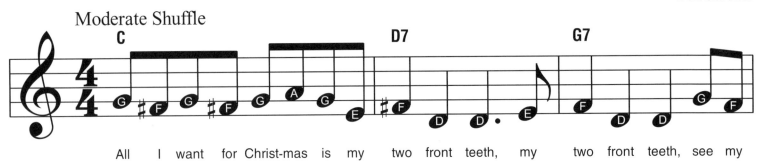

All I want for Christ-mas is my two front teeth, my two front teeth, see my

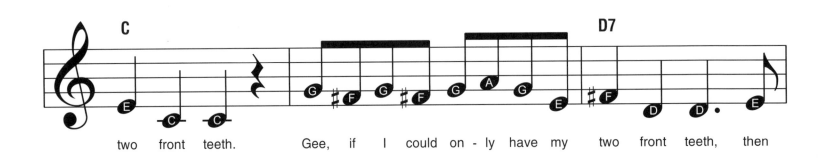

two front teeth. Gee, if I could on-ly have my two front teeth, then

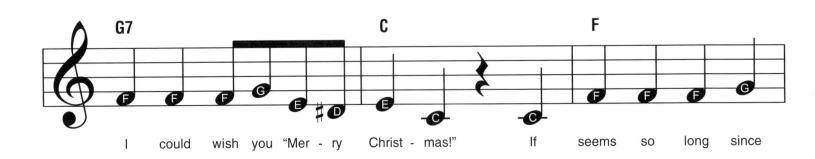

I could wish you "Mer-ry Christ-mas!" If seems so long since

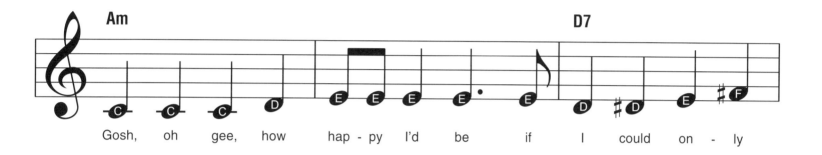

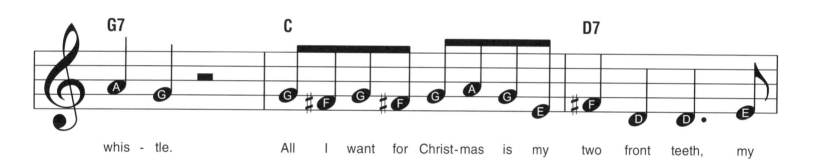

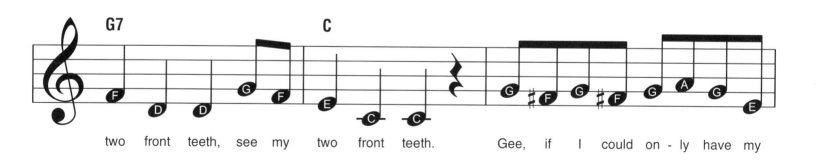

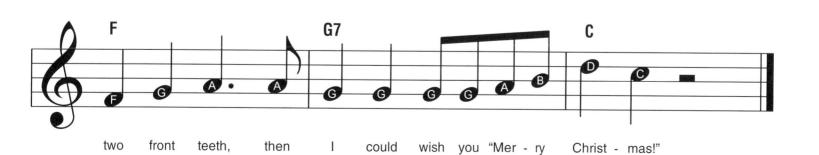

All I Want for Christmas Is You

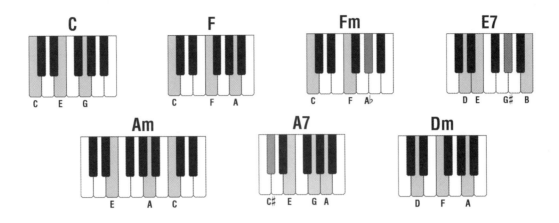

Words and Music by Mariah Carey
and Walter Afanasieff

Brightly

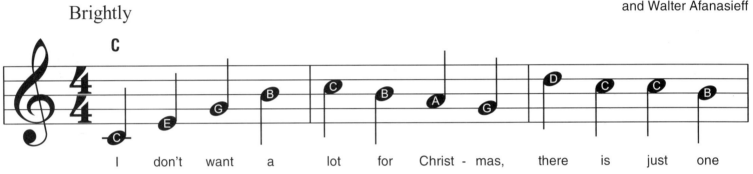

I don't want a lot for Christ-mas, there is just one

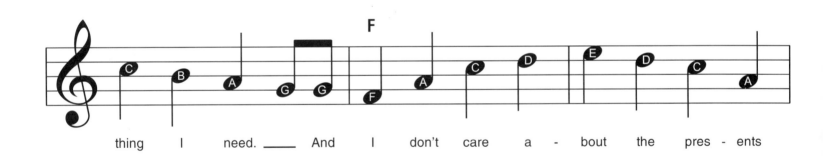

thing I need. ___ And I don't care a - bout the pres - ents

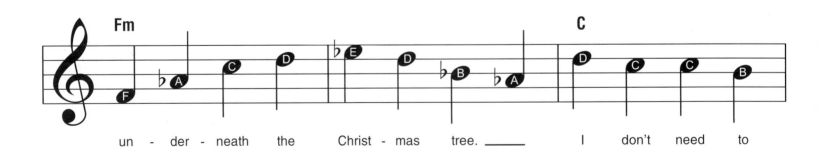

un - der - neath the Christ - mas tree. ___ I don't need to

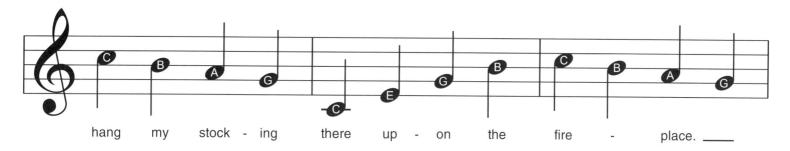

hang my stock - ing there up - on the fire - place. ____

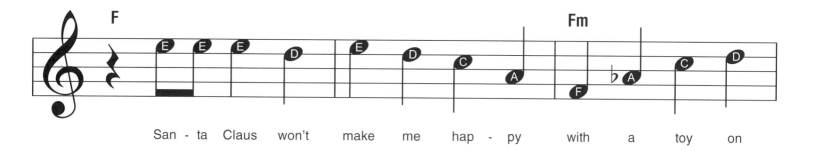

San - ta Claus won't make me hap - py with a toy on

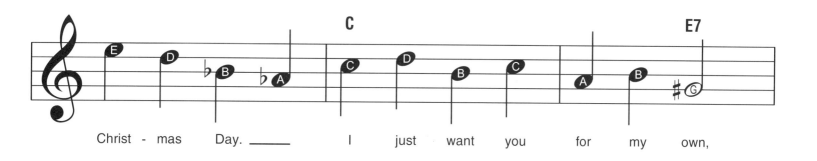

Christ - mas Day. ____ I just want you for my own,

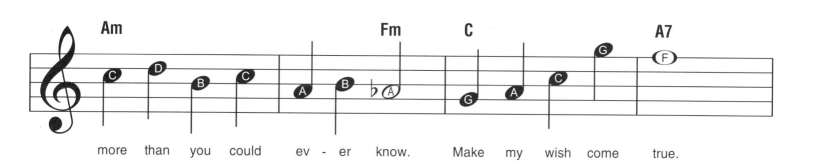

more than you could ev - er know. Make my wish come true.

All I want for Christ - mas is you. _____

Believe

from Warner Bros. Pictures' THE POLAR EXPRESS

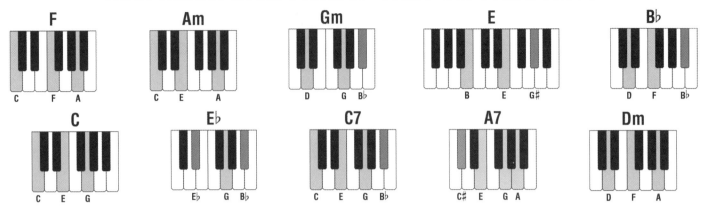

Words and Music by Glen Ballard
and Alan Silvestri

Moderately slow

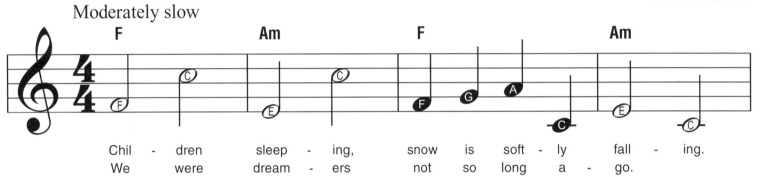

Chil- dren sleep- ing, snow is soft- ly fall- ing.
We were dream- ers not so long a - go.

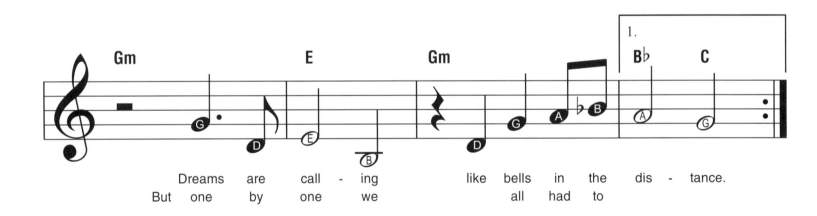

Dreams are call- ing like bells in the dis- tance.
But one by one we all had to

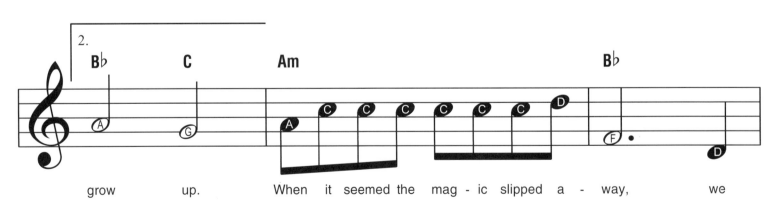

grow up. When it seemed the mag- ic slipped a - way, we

11

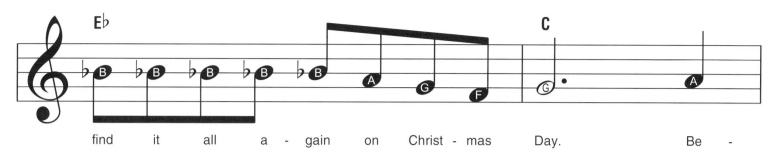

find it all a - gain on Christ - mas Day. Be -

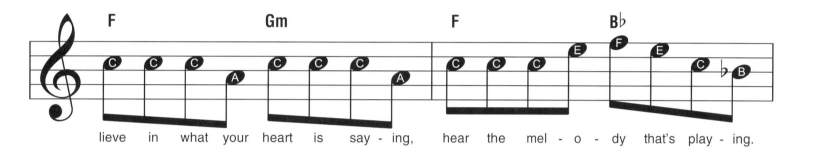

lieve in what your heart is say - ing, hear the mel - o - dy that's play - ing.

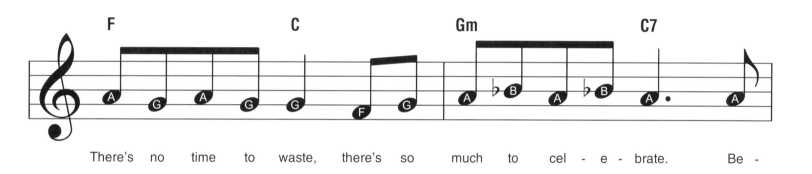

There's no time to waste, there's so much to cel - e - brate. Be -

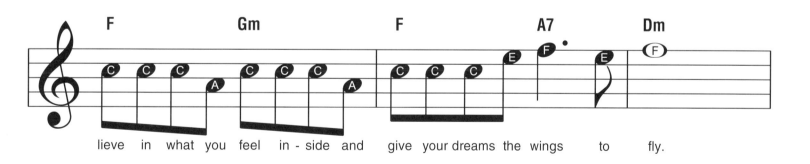

lieve in what you feel in - side and give your dreams the wings to fly.

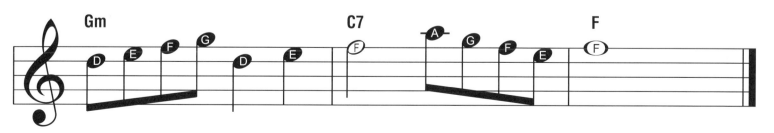

You have ev - 'ry - thing you need if you just be - lieve.

Blue Christmas

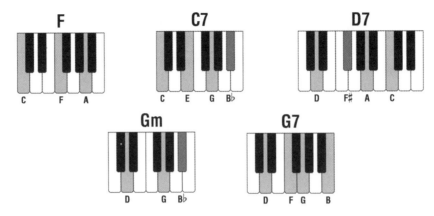

Words and Music by Billy Hayes
and Jay Johnson

Sad Shuffle

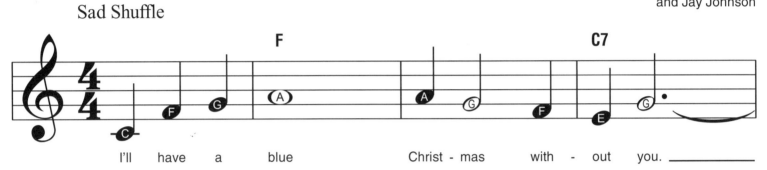

I'll have a blue Christ-mas with-out you. _____

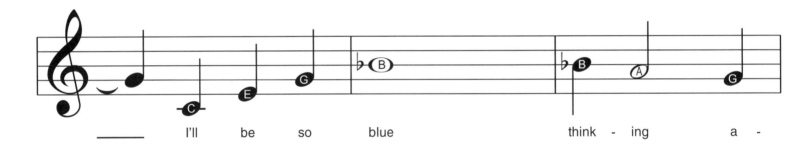

_____ I'll be so blue think-ing a-

bout you. _____ Dec-o-ra-tions of

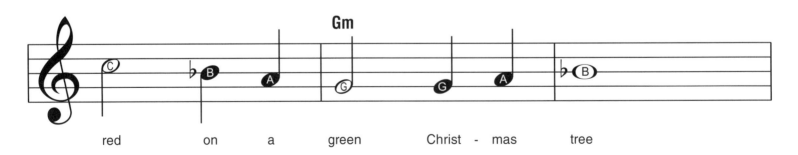

red on a green Christ-mas tree

13

C-H-R-I-S-T-M-A-S

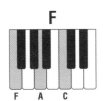
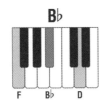
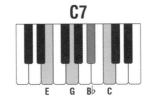

Words by Jenny Lou Carson
Music by Eddy Arnold

Brightly

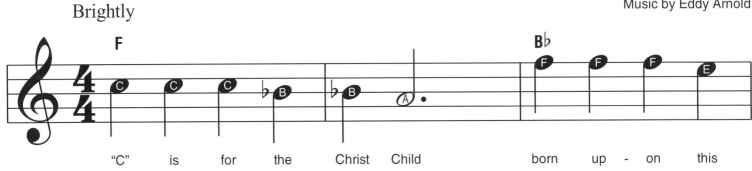

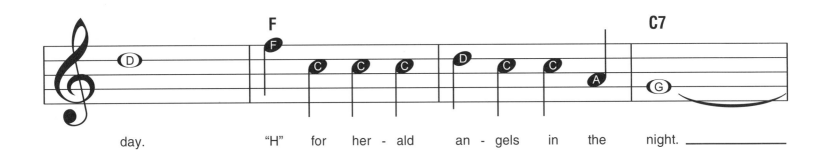

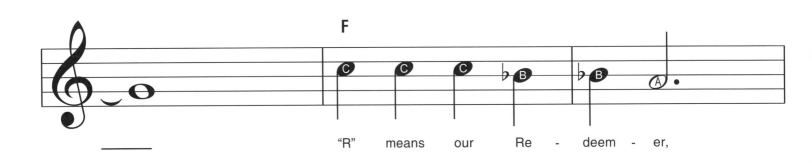

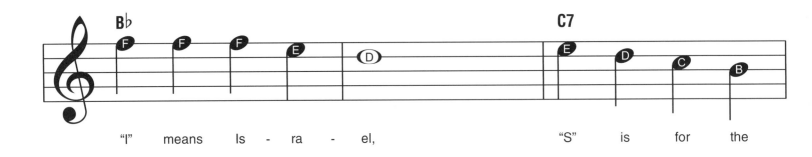

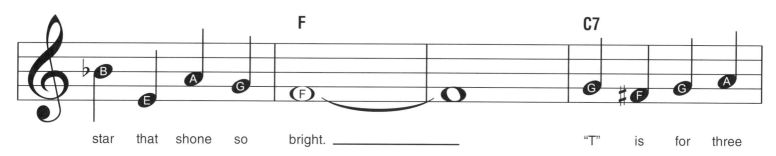

star that shone so bright. _____ "T" is for three

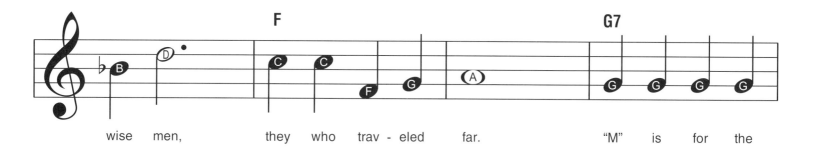

wise men, they who trav - eled far. "M" is for the

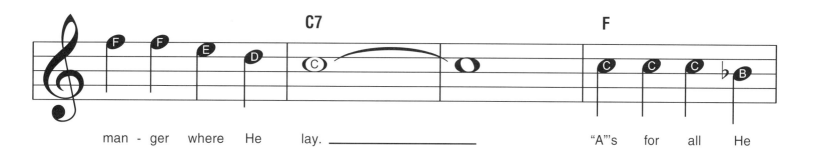

man - ger where He lay. _____ "A"'s for all He

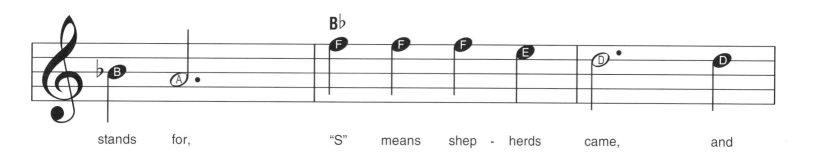

stands for, "S" means shep - herds came, and

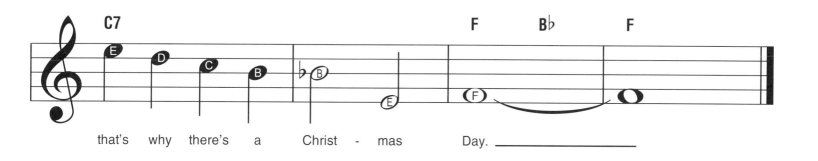

that's why there's a Christ - mas Day. _____

Caroling, Caroling

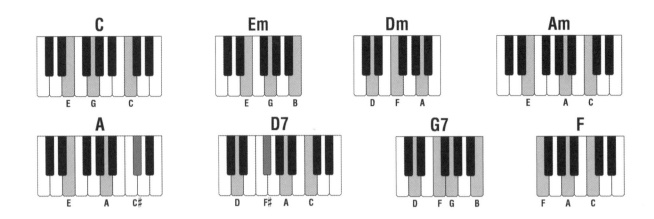

Words by Wihla Hutson
Music by Alfred Burt

Moderately fast

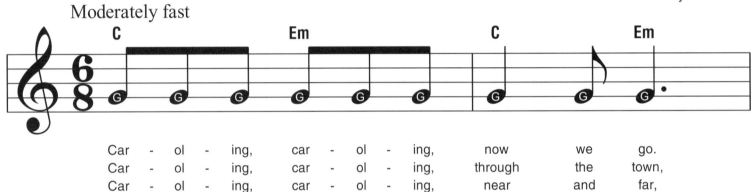

Car	-	ol	-	ing,	car	-	ol	-	ing,	now	we	go.
Car	-	ol	-	ing,	car	-	ol	-	ing,	through	the	town,
Car	-	ol	-	ing,	car	-	ol	-	ing,	near	and	far,

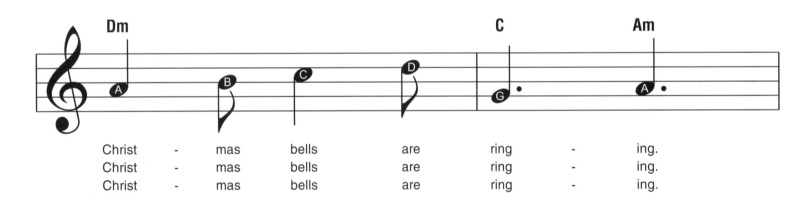

Christ	-	mas	bells	are	ring	-	ing.
Christ	-	mas	bells	are	ring	-	ing.
Christ	-	mas	bells	are	ring	-	ing.

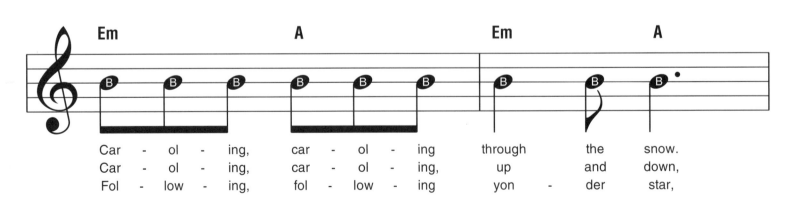

Car	-	ol	-	ing,	car	-	ol	-	ing	through	the	snow.
Car	-	ol	-	ing,	car	-	ol	-	ing,	up	and	down,
Fol	-	low	-	ing,	fol	-	low	-	ing	yon	-	der	star,

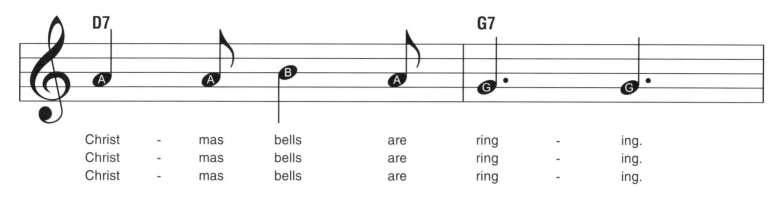

Christ - mas bells are ring - ing.
Christ - mas bells are ring - ing.
Christ - mas bells are ring - ing.

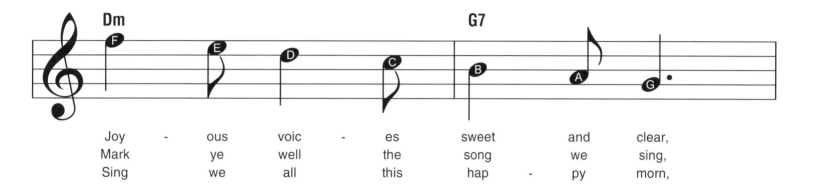

Joy - ous voic - es sweet and clear,
Mark ye well the song we sing,
Sing we all this hap - py morn,

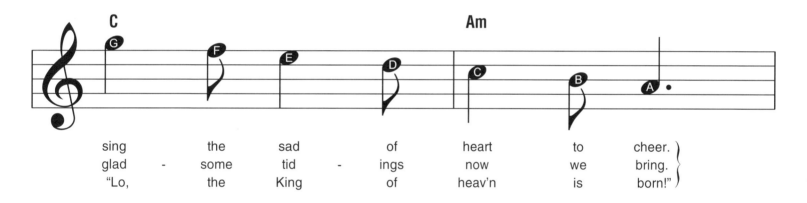

sing the sad of heart to cheer.
glad - some tid - ings now we bring.
"Lo, the King of heav'n is born!"

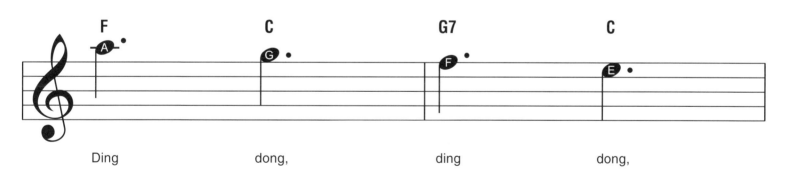

Ding dong, ding dong,

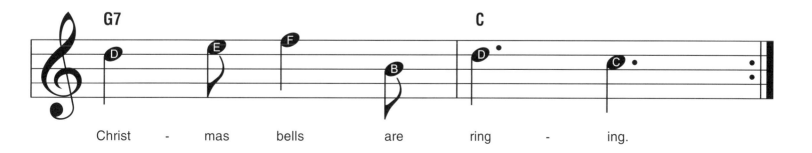

Christ - mas bells are ring - ing.

A Child Is Born

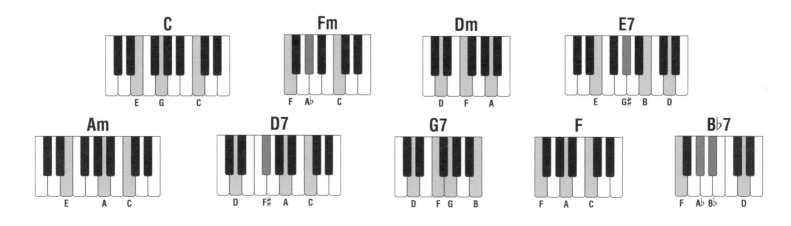

Music by Thad Jones
Lyrics by Alec Wilder

Gently

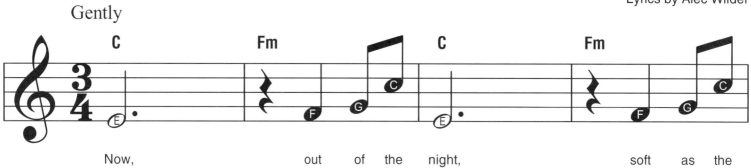

Now, out of the night, soft as the

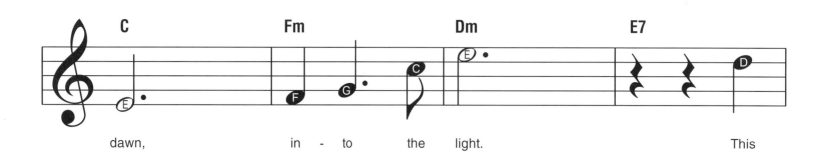

dawn, in - to the light. This

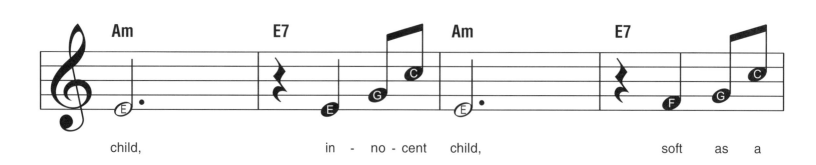

child, in - no - cent child, soft as a

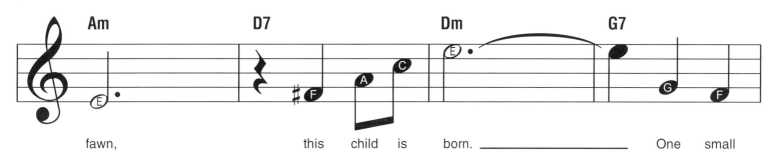

fawn, this child is born. _____ One small

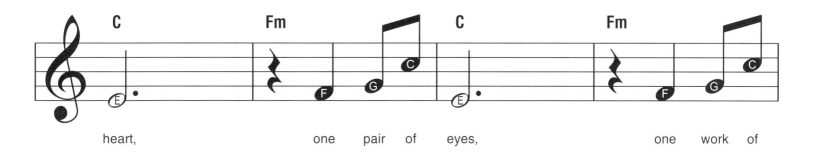

heart, one pair of eyes, one work of

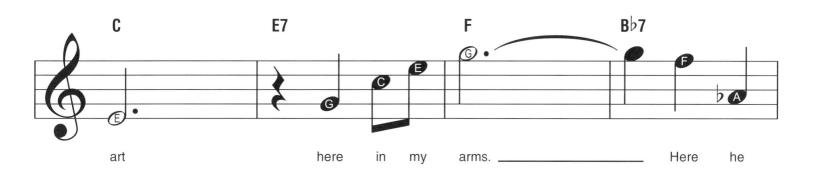

art here in my arms. _____ Here he

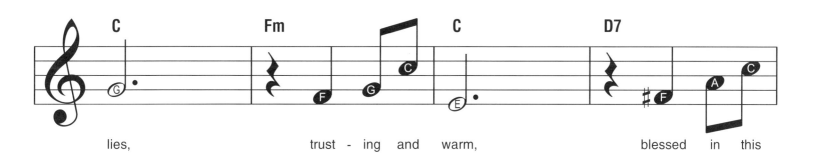

lies, trust-ing and warm, blessed in this

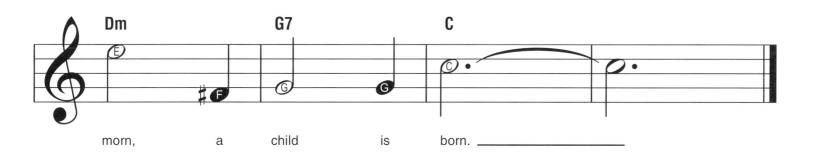

morn, a child is born. _____

The Chipmunk Song

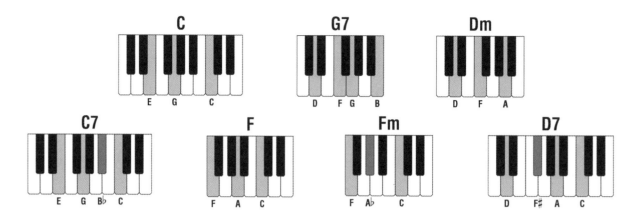

Words and Music by
Ross Bagdasarian

Moderate Waltz

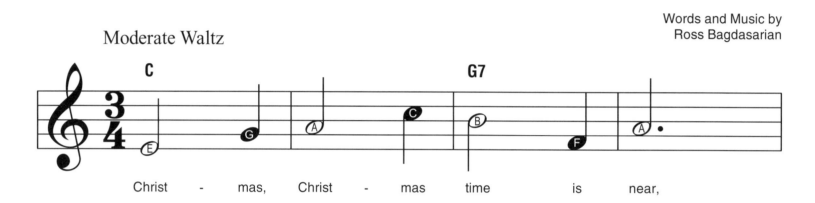

Christ - mas, Christ - mas time is near,

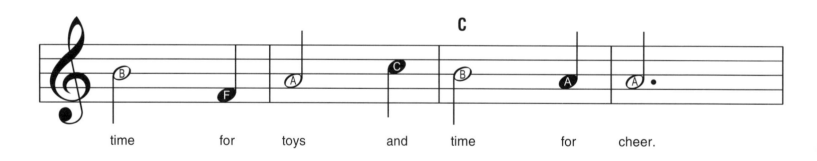

time for toys and time for cheer.

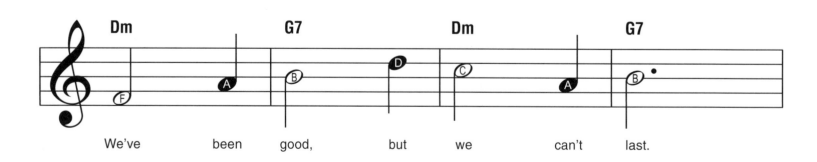

We've been good, but we can't last.

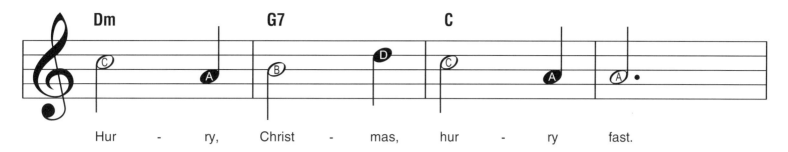

Hur - ry, Christ - mas, hur - ry fast.

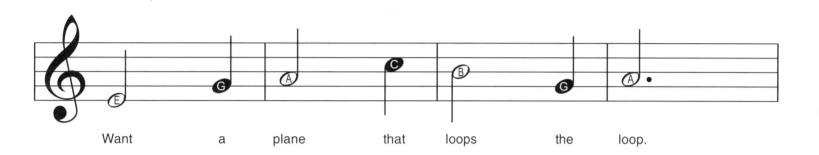

Want a plane that loops the loop.

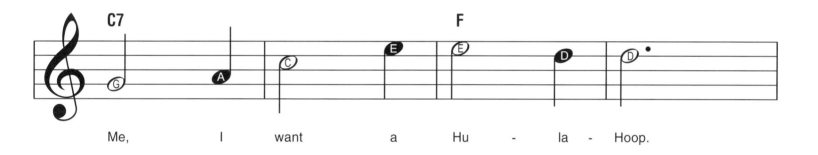

Me, I want a Hu - la - Hoop.

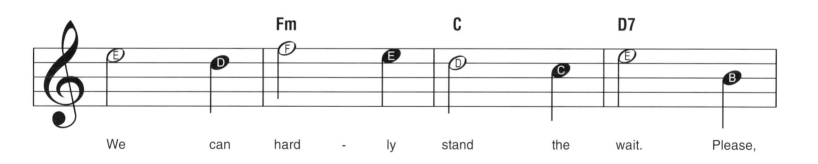

We can hard - ly stand the wait. Please,

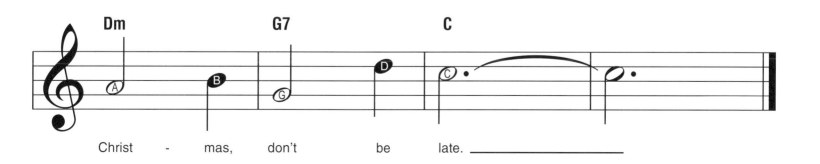

Christ - mas, don't be late. _____

Christmas Is

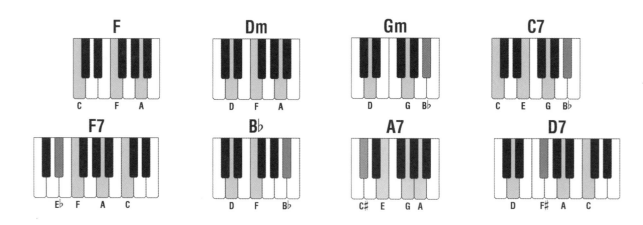

Lyrics by Spence Maxwell
Music by Percy Faith

Moderate Shuffle

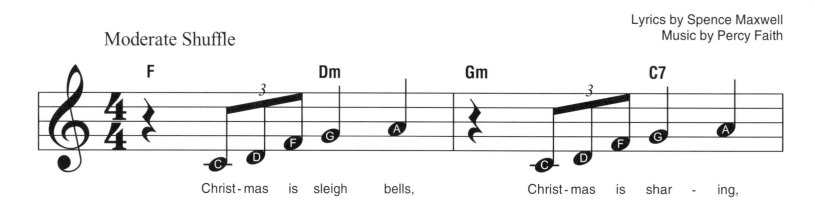

Christ - mas is sleigh bells, Christ - mas is shar - ing,

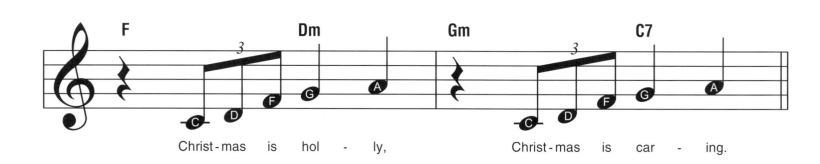

Christ - mas is hol - ly, Christ - mas is car - ing.

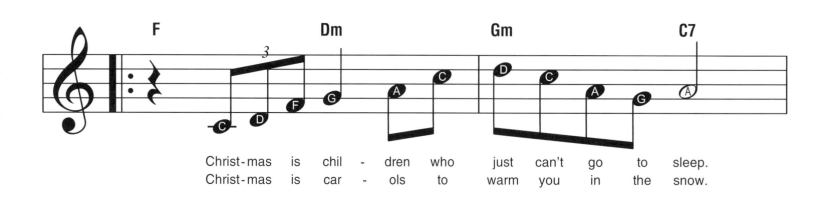

Christ - mas is chil - dren who just can't go to sleep.
Christ - mas is car - ols to warm you in the snow.

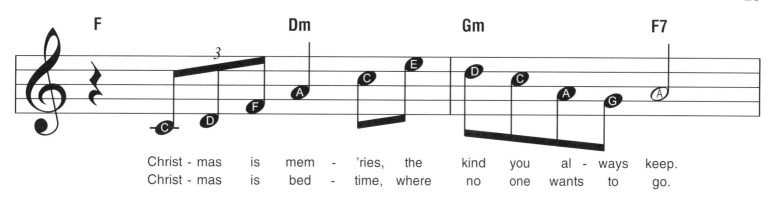

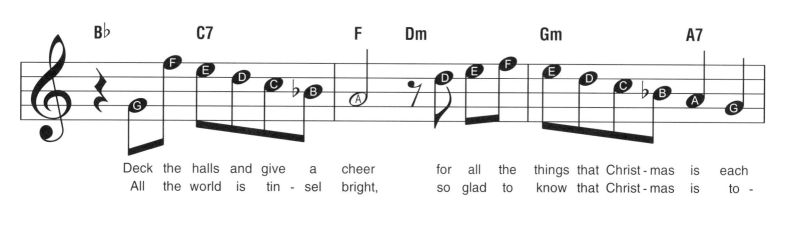

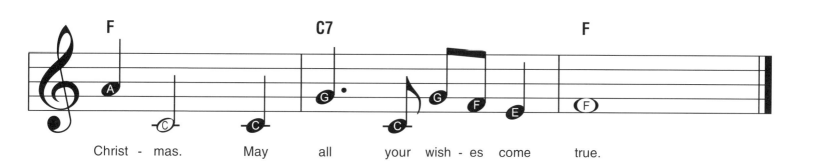

Christmas Is A-Comin'
(May God Bless You)

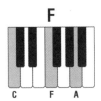 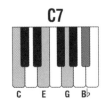 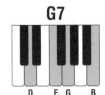 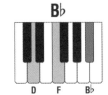

Words and Music by
Frank Luther

Moderate Shuffle

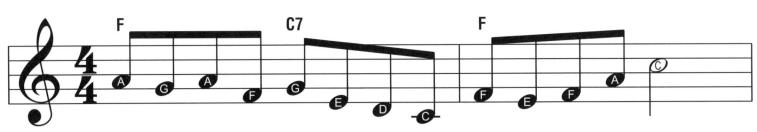

Christ - mas is a - com - in' and the geese are get - tin' fat.

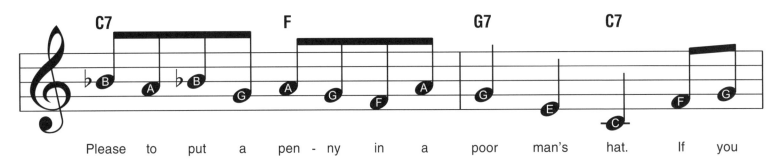

Please to put a pen - ny in a poor man's hat. If you

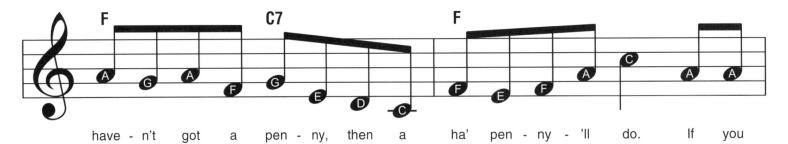

have - n't got a pen - ny, then a ha' pen - ny - 'll do. If you

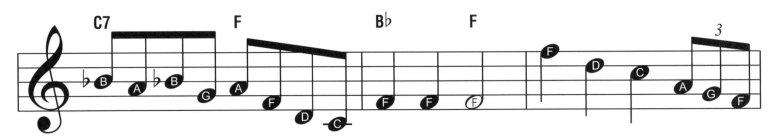

have - n't got a ha' pen - ny, may God bless you. God bless you, gen - tle - men,

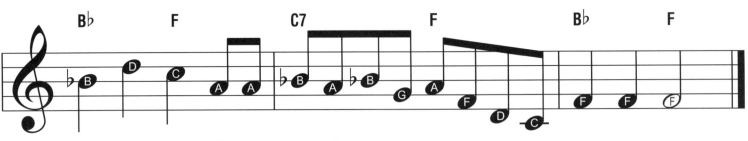

God bless you. If you have - n't got a ha' pen - ny, may God bless you.

Happy Holiday

from the Motion Picture Irving Berlin's HOLIDAY INN

Words and Music by
Irving Berlin

Bright Shuffle

Hap - py hol - i - day, _____ hap - py hol - i - day. _____

_____ While the mer - ry bells keep ring - ing, may your

ev - 'ry wish come true. Hap - py hol - i - day, _____

_____ hap - py hol - i - day. _____ May the

cal - en - dar keep bring - ing hap - py hol - i - days to you.

The Christmas Song
(Chestnuts Roasting on an Open Fire)

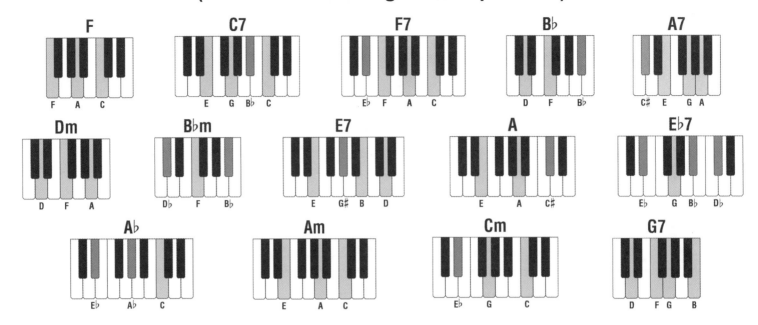

Music and Lyric by Mel Tormé
and Robert Wells

Chest - nuts roast - ing on an o - pen fire, Jack Frost nip - ping at your
knows a tur - key and some mis - tle - toe help to make the sea - son

nose. Yule - tide car - ols be - ing sung by a choir and
bright. Ti - ny tots ___ with their eyes all a - glow will

folks dressed up like Es - ki - mos. Ev - 'ry - bod - y
find it hard to sleep to -

Christmas Time Is Here

from A CHARLIE BROWN CHRISTMAS

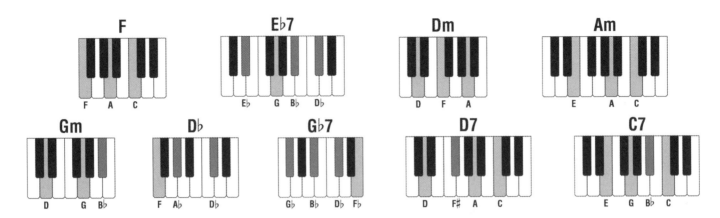

Words by Lee Mendelson
Music by Vince Guaraldi

Moderately

Christ - mas time is here, happi - ness and
Snow - flakes in the air, car - ols ev - 'ry -

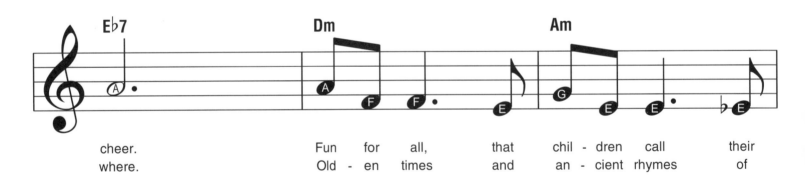

cheer. Fun for all, that chil - dren call their
where. Old - en times and an - cient rhymes of

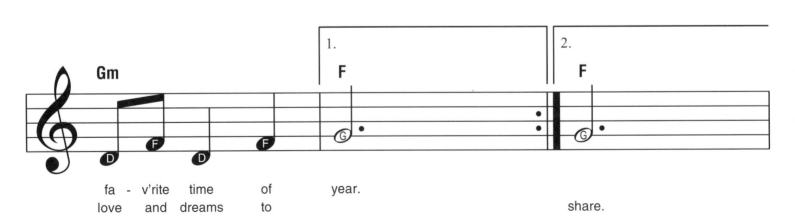

fa - v'rite time of year.
love and dreams to share.

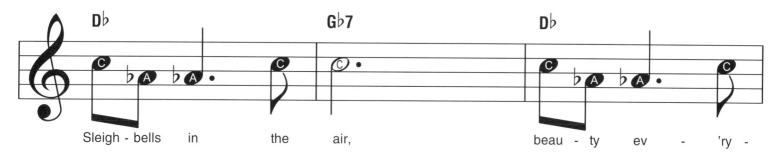

Sleigh - bells in the air, beau - ty ev - 'ry -

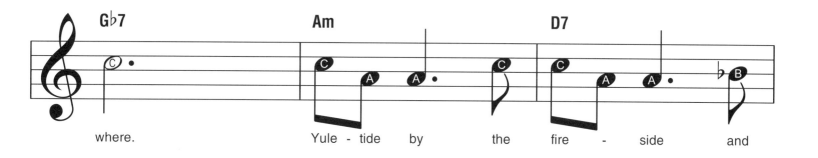

where. Yule - tide by the fire - side and

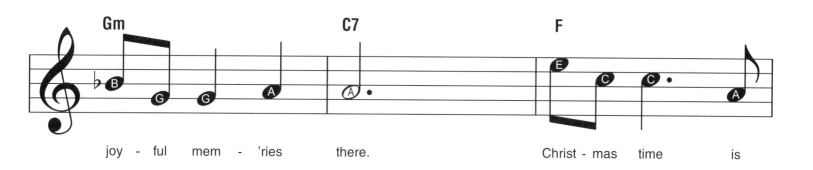

joy - ful mem - 'ries there. Christ - mas time is

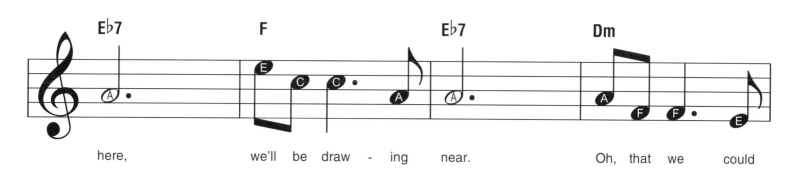

here, we'll be draw - ing near. Oh, that we could

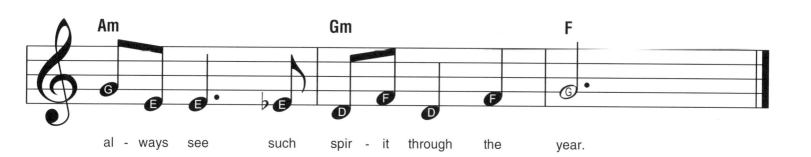

al - ways see such spir - it through the year.

The Christmas Waltz

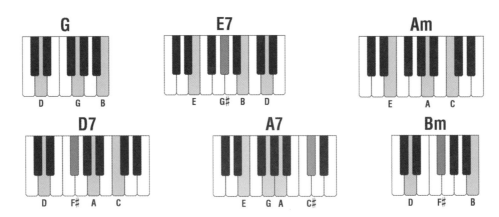

Words by Sammy Cahn
Music by Jule Styne

Lilting

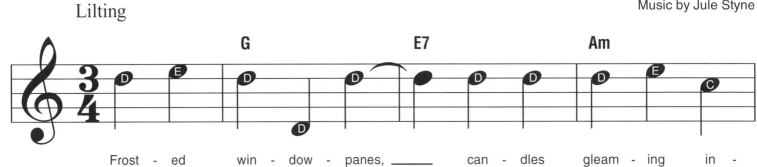

Frost - ed win - dow - panes, _____ can - dles gleam - ing in -

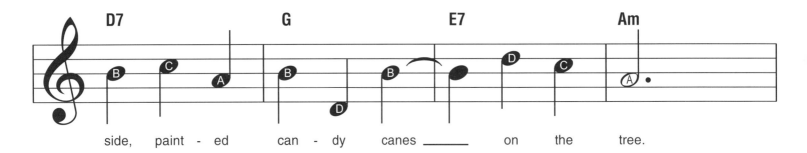

side, paint - ed can - dy canes _____ on the tree.

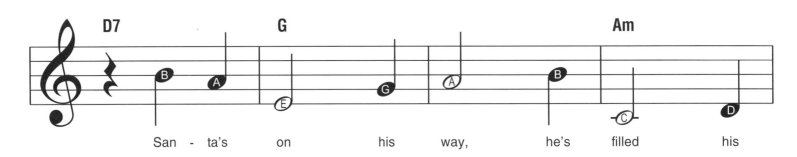

San - ta's on his way, he's filled his

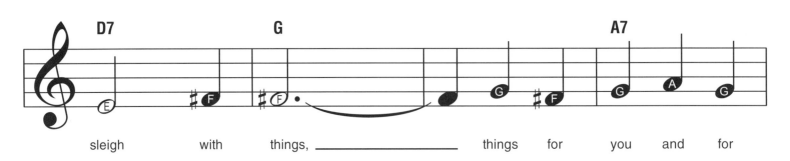

sleigh with things, _____ things for you and for

31

Do They Know It's Christmas?
(Feed the World)

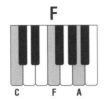 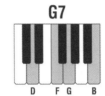 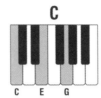 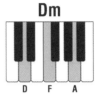

Words and Music by Bob Geldof
and Midge Ure

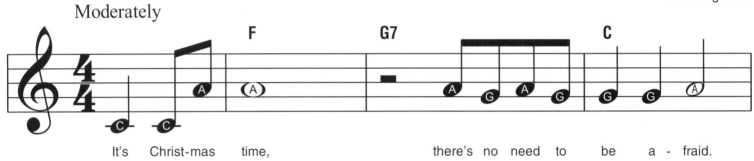

It's Christ-mas time, there's no need to be a - fraid.

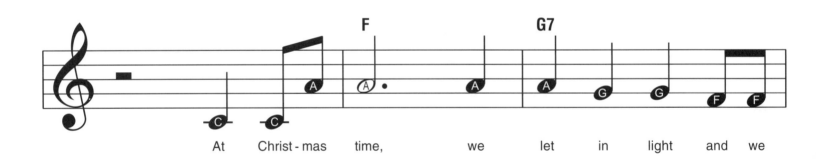

At Christ-mas time, we let in light and we

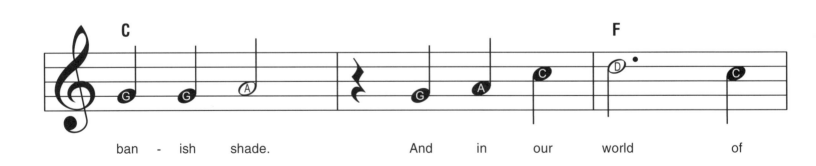

ban - ish shade. And in our world of

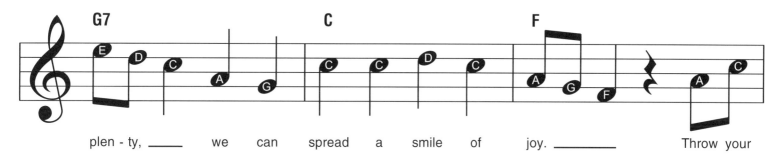

plen - ty, _____ we can spread a smile of joy. _____ Throw your

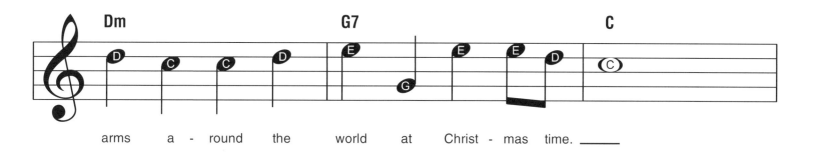

arms a - round the world at Christ - mas time. _____

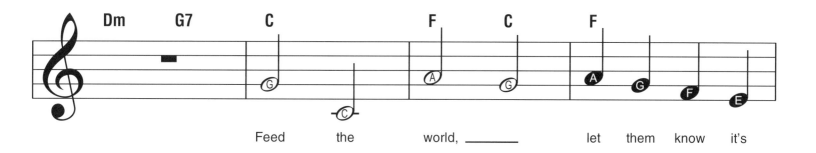

Feed the world, _____ let them know it's

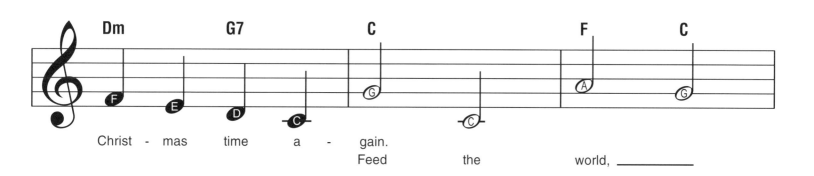

Christ - mas time a - gain.
Feed the world, _____

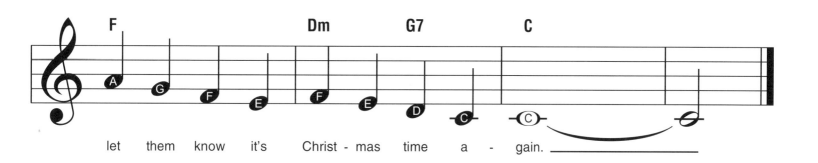

let them know it's Christ - mas time a - gain. _____

Do You Hear What I Hear

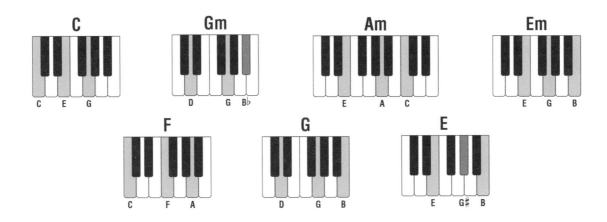

Words and Music by Noel Regney
and Gloria Shayne

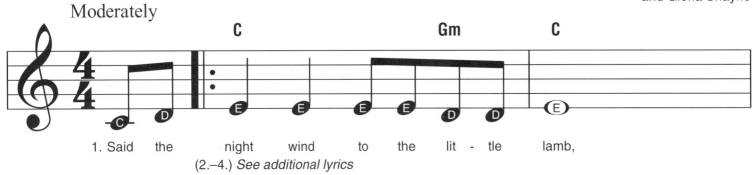

1. Said the night wind to the lit - tle lamb,
(2.–4.) *See additional lyrics*

"Do you see what I see? _____ Way up in the sky, lit - tle

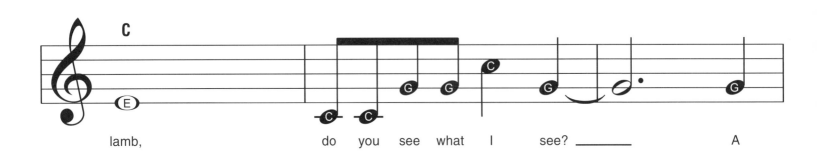

lamb, do you see what I see? _____ A

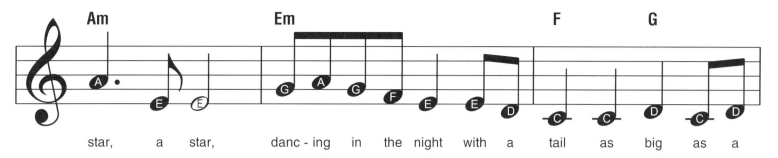

star,   a star,   danc - ing   in   the   night   with   a   tail   as   big   as   a

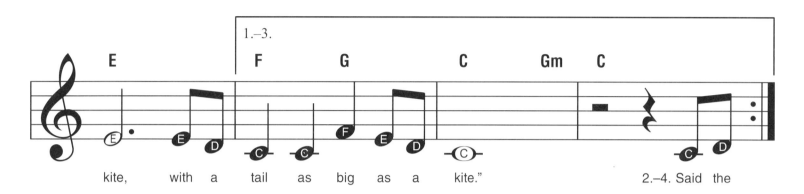

kite,   with   a   tail   as   big   as   a   kite."   2.–4. Said   the

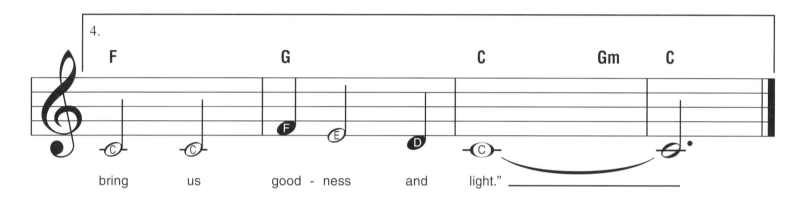

bring   us   good - ness   and   light." _____

Additional Lyrics

2. Said the little lamb to the shepherd boy,
   "Do you hear what I hear?
   Ringing through the sky, shepherd boy,
   Do you hear what I hear?
   A song, a song, high above the tree,
   With a voice as big as the sea,
   With a voice as big as the sea."

3. Said the shepherd boy to the mighty king,
   "Do you know what I know?
   In your palace warm, mighty king,
   Do you know what I know?
   A Child, a Child shivers in the cold;
   Let us bring Him silver and gold,
   Let us bring Him silver and gold."

4. Said the king to the people everywhere,
   "LIsten to what I say!
   Pray for peace, people everywhere.
   Listen to what I say!
   The Child, the Child, sleeping in the night,
   He will bring us goodness and light,
   He will bring us goodness and light."

Do You Want to Build a Snowman?

from FROZEN

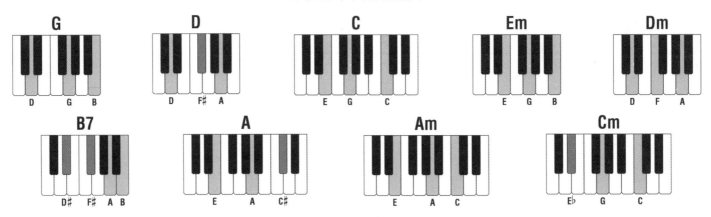

Music and Lyrics by Kristen Anderson-Lopez
and Robert Lopez

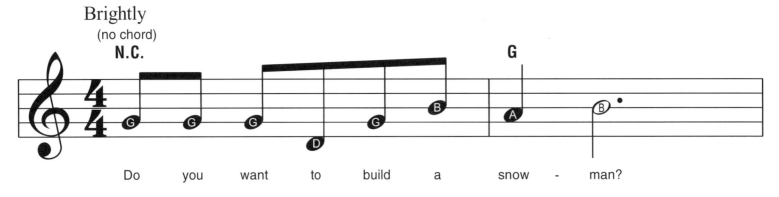

Do you want to build a snow - man?

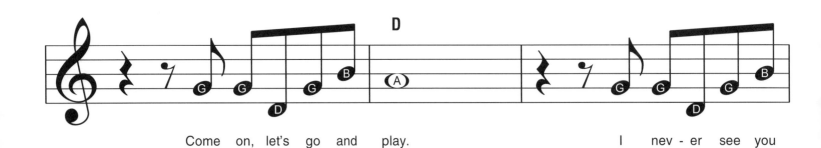

Come on, let's go and play.   I nev - er see you

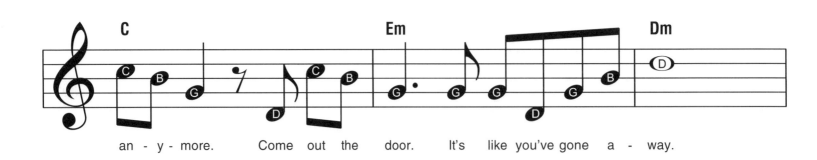

an - y - more.   Come out the door.   It's like you've gone a - way.

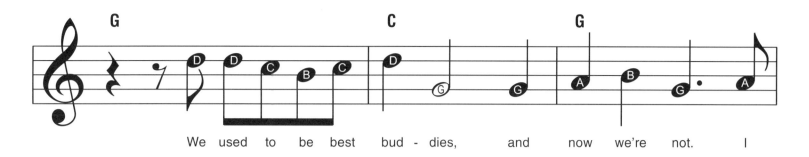

G   C   G

We used to be best bud - dies, and now we're not. I

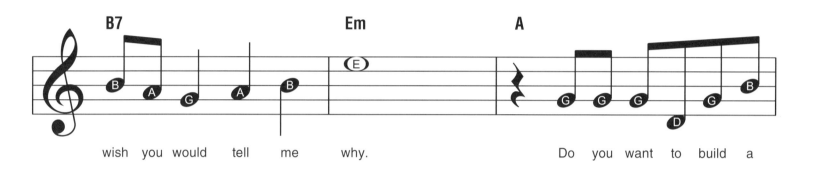

B7   Em   A

wish you would tell me why. Do you want to build a

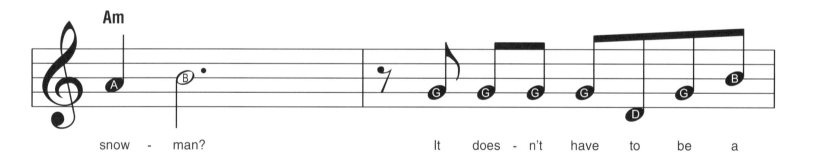

Am

snow - man? It does - n't have to be a

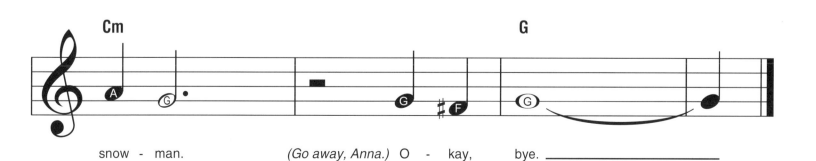

Cm   G

snow - man. *(Go away, Anna.)* O - kay, bye. _____

Fairytale of New York

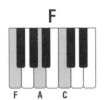
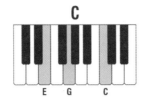
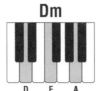
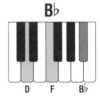

Words and Music by Jeremy Finer
and Shane MacGowan

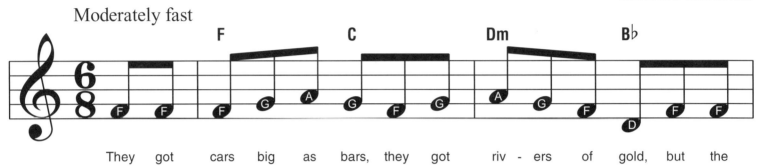

They got cars big as bars, they got riv-ers of gold, but the

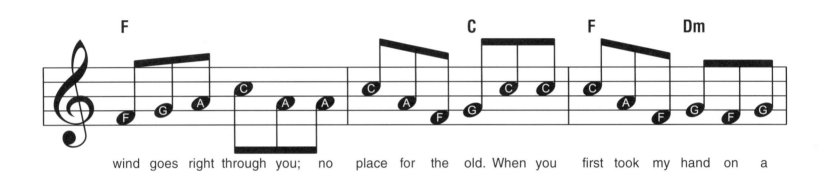

wind goes right through you; no place for the old. When you first took my hand on a

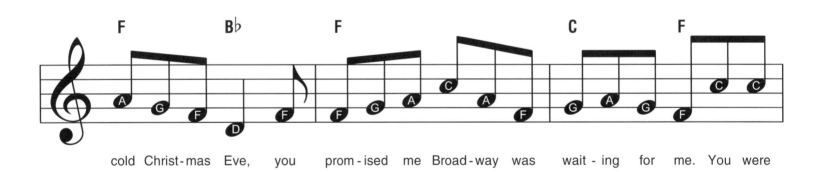

cold Christ-mas Eve, you prom-ised me Broad-way was wait-ing for me. You were

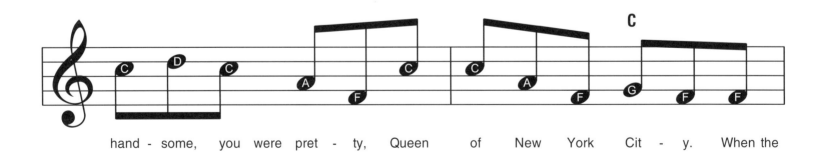

hand-some, you were pret-ty, Queen of New York Cit-y. When the

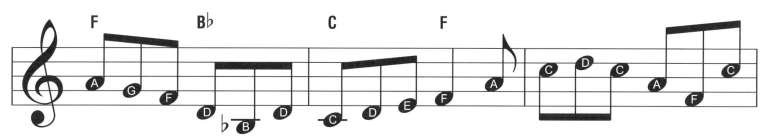

band fin - ished play - ing, they howled out for more. Si - na - tra was swing - ing, the

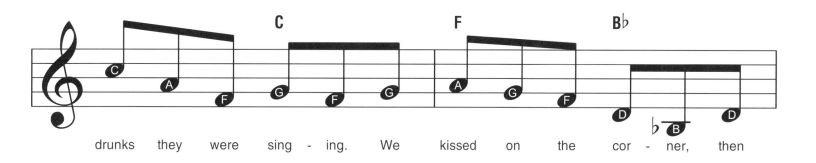

drunks they were sing - ing. We kissed on the cor - ner, then

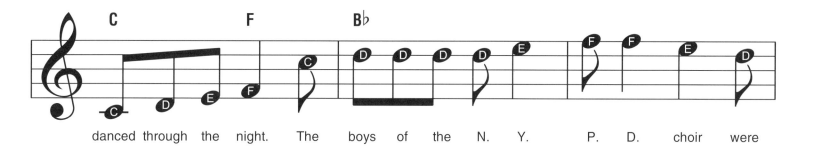

danced through the night. The boys of the N. Y. P. D. choir were

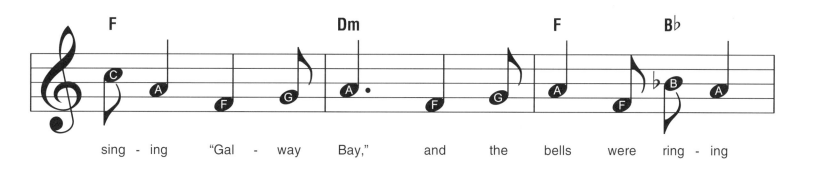

sing - ing "Gal - way Bay," and the bells were ring - ing

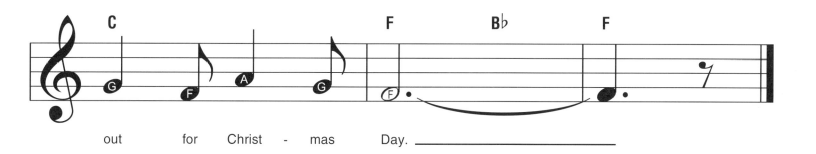

out for Christ - mas Day. _____

Feliz Navidad

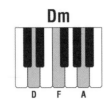
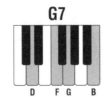
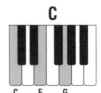
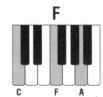

Music and Lyrics by
José Feliciano

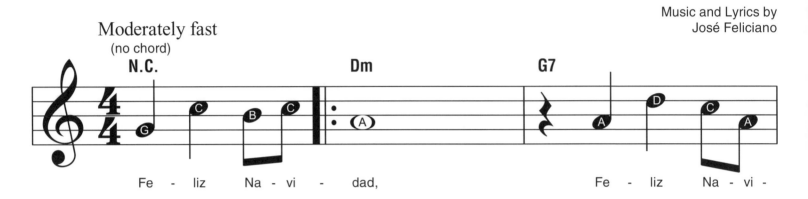

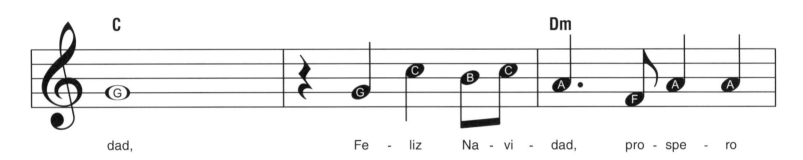

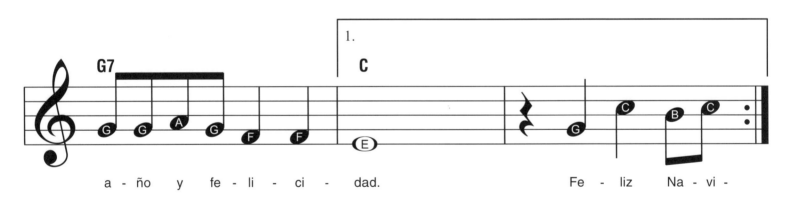

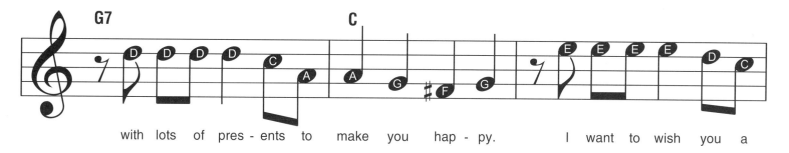

with lots of pres - ents to make you hap - py. I want to wish you a

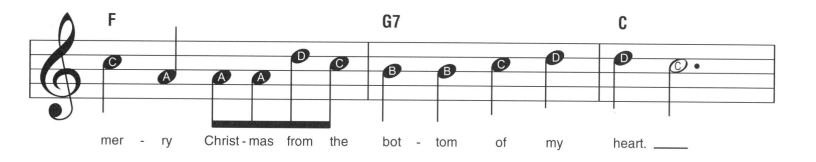

mer - ry Christ - mas from the bot - tom of my heart. ____

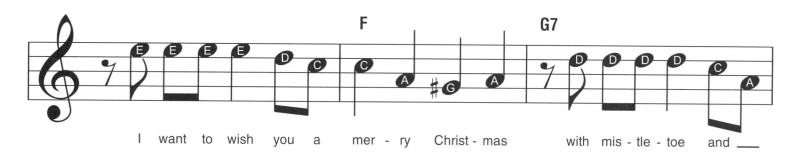

I want to wish you a mer - ry Christ - mas with mis - tle - toe and ___

lots of cheer, _____ with lots of laugh - ter through -

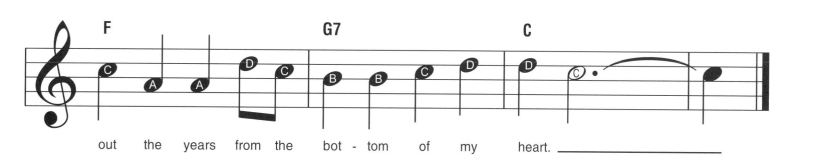

out the years from the bot - tom of my heart. _____

Frosty the Snow Man

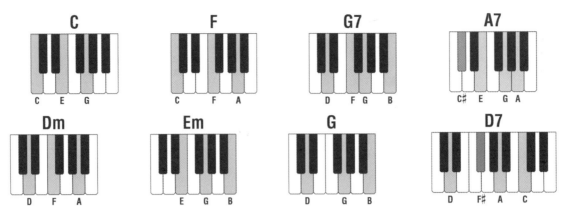

Words and Music by Steve Nelson
and Jack Rollins

Moderately fast

Frost - y the Snow Man was a jol - ly, hap - py
Frost - y the Snow Man knew the sun was hot that

soul, with a corn - cob pipe and a but - ton nose and two
day, so he said, "Let's run and we'll have some fun now be -

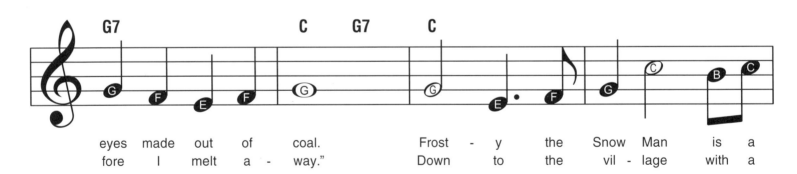

eyes made out of coal. Frost - y the Snow Man is a
fore I melt a - way." Down to the vil - lage with a

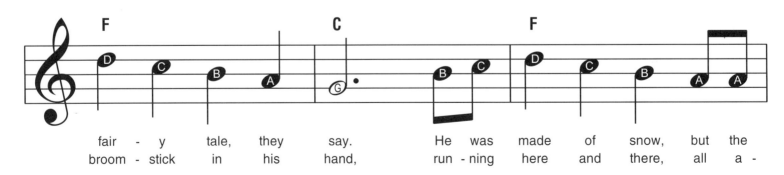

fair - y tale, they say. He was made of snow, but the
broom - stick in his hand, run - ning here and there, all a -

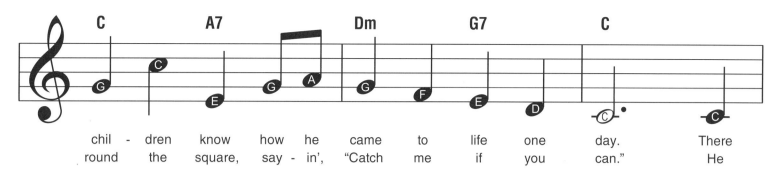

chil - dren know how he came to life one day. There
round the square, say - in', "Catch me if you can." He

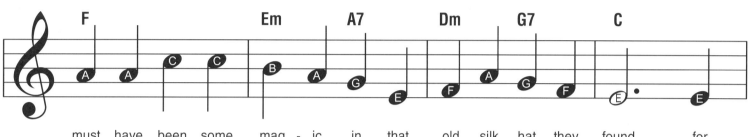

must have been some mag - ic in that old silk hat they found, for
led them down the streets of town right to the traf - fic cop, and he

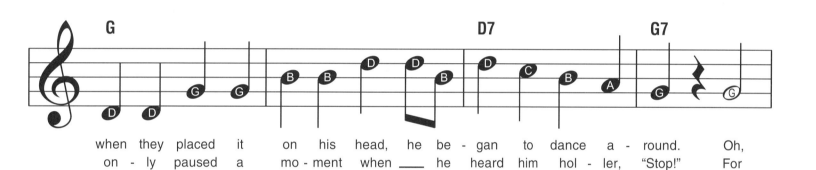

when they placed it on his head, he be - gan to dance a - round. Oh,
on - ly paused a mo - ment when ___ he heard him hol - ler, "Stop!" For

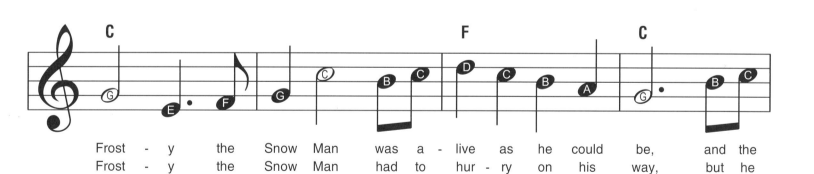

Frost - y the Snow Man was a - live as he could be, and the
Frost - y the Snow Man had to hur - ry on his way, but he

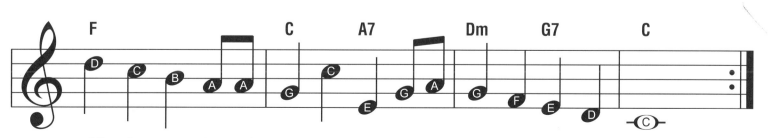

chil - dren say he could laugh and play just the same as you and me.
waved good - bye, say - in', "Don't you cry. I'll be back a - gain some - day."

Grandma Got Run Over by a Reindeer

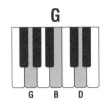 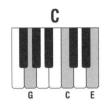  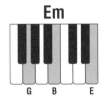 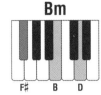

Words and Music by
Randy Brooks

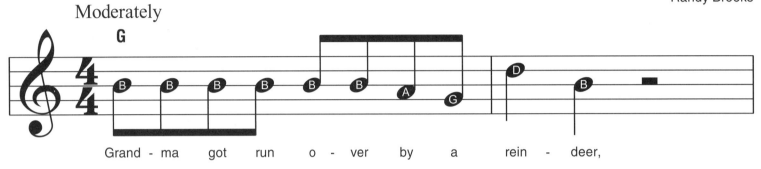

Grand - ma got run o - ver by a rein - deer,

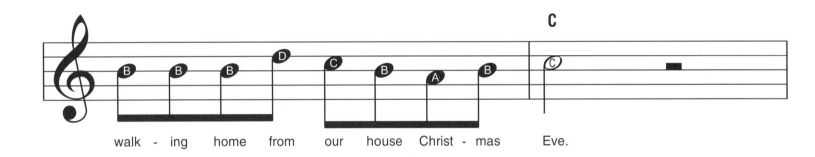

walk - ing home from our house Christ - mas Eve.

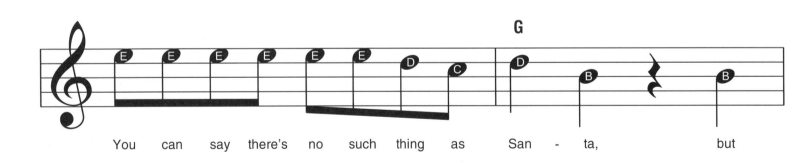

You can say there's no such thing as San - ta, but

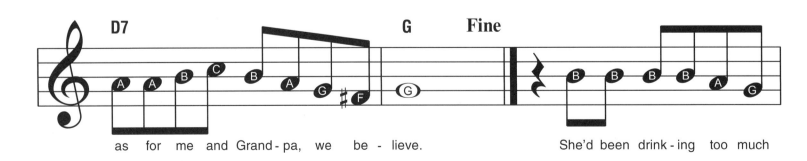

as for me and Grand - pa, we be - lieve. She'd been drink - ing too much

egg - nog, and we begged her not to go.

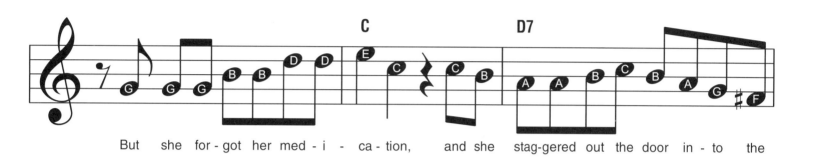

But she for-got her med - i - ca - tion, and she stag-gered out the door in - to the

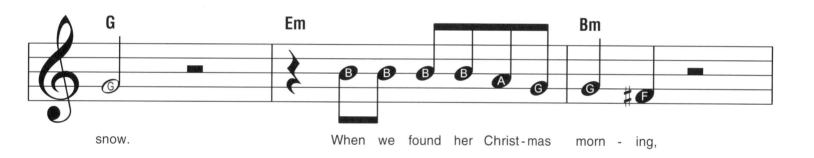

snow. When we found her Christ-mas morn - ing,

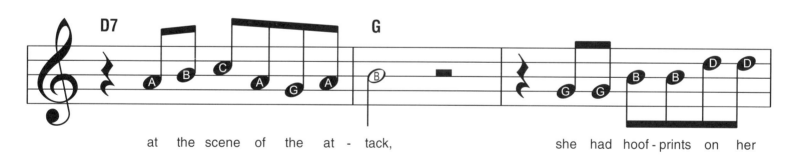

at the scene of the at - tack, she had hoof - prints on her

D.C. al Fine
(Return to beginning
and play to Fine)

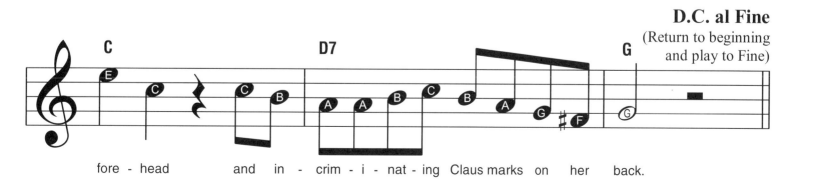

fore - head and in - crim - i - nat - ing Claus marks on her back.

Grown-Up Christmas List

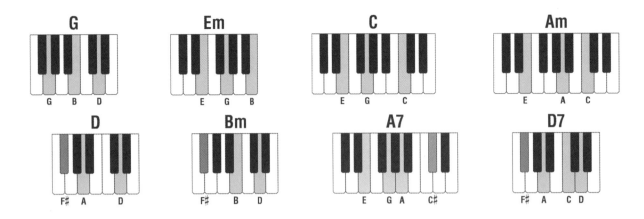

Words and Music by David Foster
and Linda Thompson-Jenner

Moderately slow

Do you re-mem-ber me? I sat up-on your knee. I
I'm all grown up now and still need help some-how. I'm

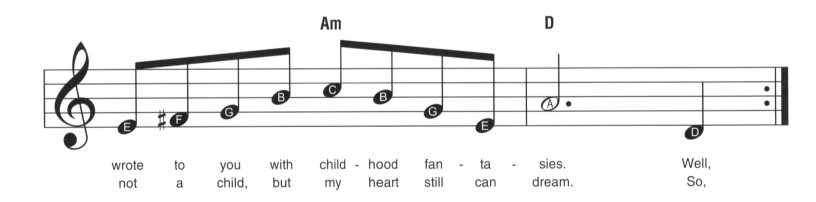

wrote to you with child-hood fan-ta- sies. Well,
not a child, but my heart still can dream. So,

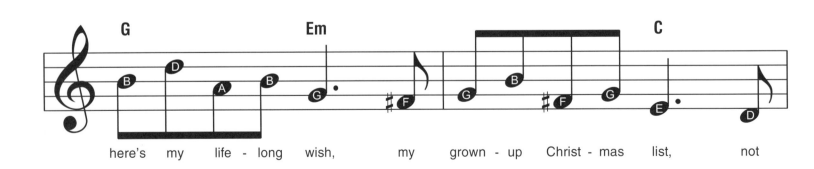

here's my life-long wish, my grown-up Christ-mas list, not

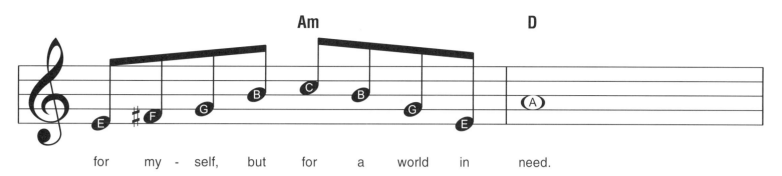

for my-self, but for a world in need.

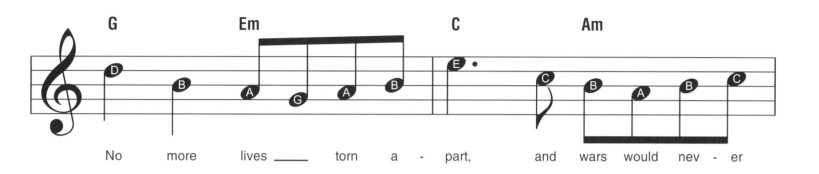

No more lives ____ torn a - part, and wars would nev - er

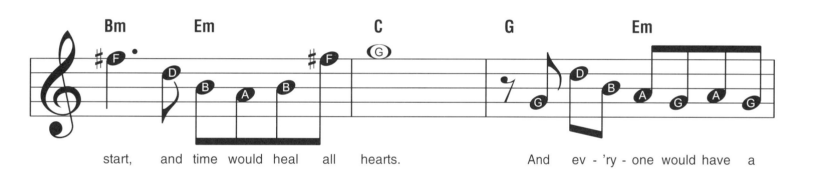

start, and time would heal all hearts. And ev - 'ry - one would have a

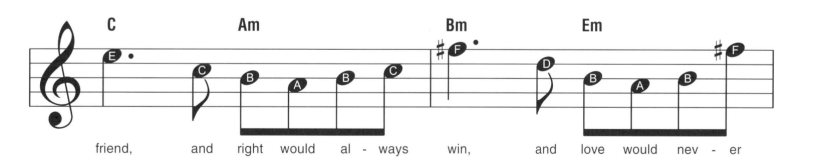

friend, and right would al - ways win, and love would nev - er

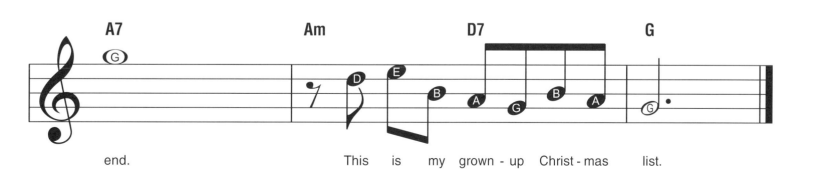

end. This is my grown - up Christ - mas list.

Happy Xmas
(War Is Over)

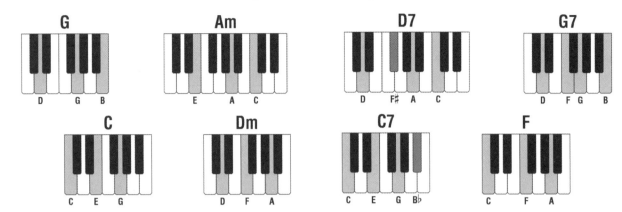

Written by John Lennon
and Yoko Ono

Moderately slow

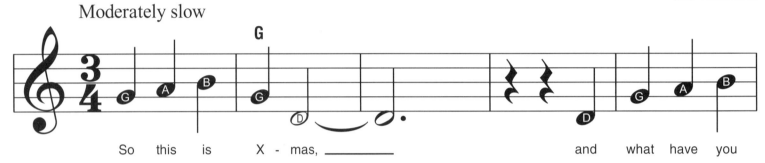

So this is X - mas, _____ and what have you

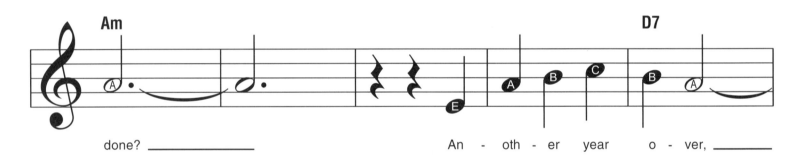

done? _____ An - oth - er year o - ver, _____

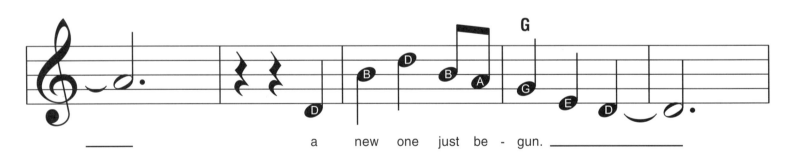

_____ a new one just be - gun. _____

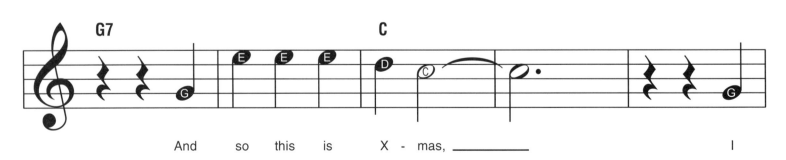

And so this is X - mas, _____ I

Have Yourself a Merry Little Christmas

from MEET ME IN ST. LOUIS

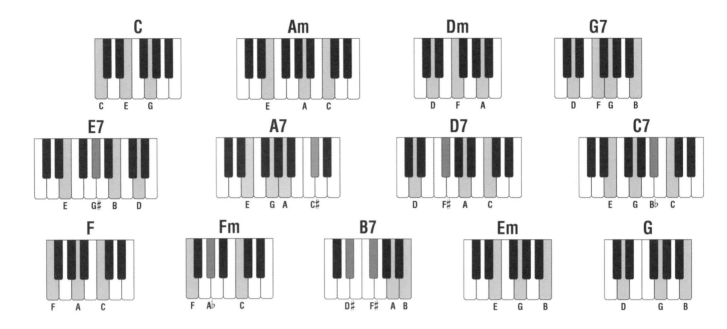

Words and Music by Hugh Martin
and Ralph Blane

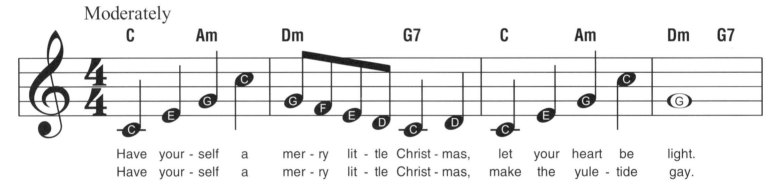

Moderately

Have your-self a mer-ry lit-tle Christ-mas, let your heart be light.
Have your-self a mer-ry lit-tle Christ-mas, make the yule-tide gay.

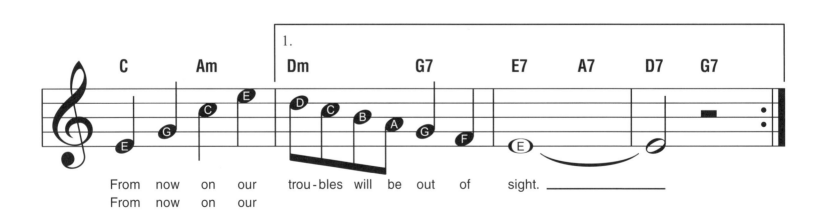

From now on our trou-bles will be out of sight. _____
From now on our

Here Comes Santa Claus
(Right Down Santa Claus Lane)

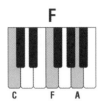 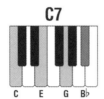 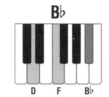 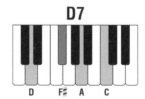 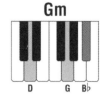

Words and Music by Gene Autry
and Oakley Haldeman

Here comes San - ta Claus! Here comes San - ta Claus! Right down Santa Claus

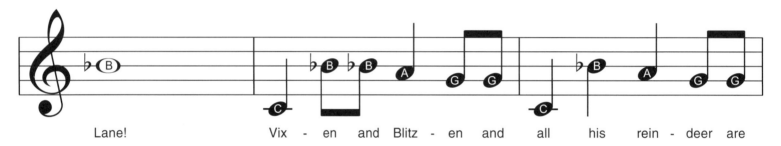

Lane! Vix - en and Blitz - en and all his rein - deer are

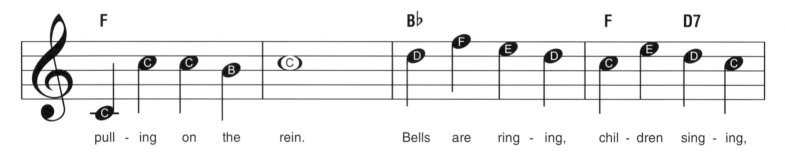

pull - ing on the rein. Bells are ring - ing, chil - dren sing - ing,

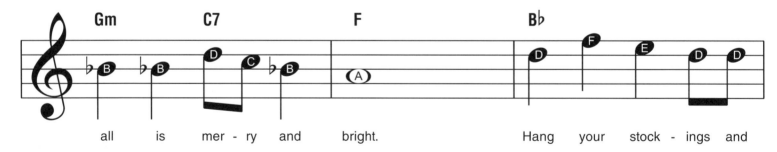

all is mer - ry and bright. Hang your stock - ings and

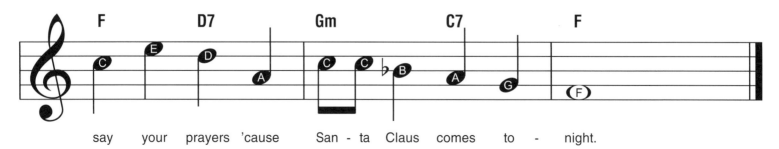

say your prayers 'cause San - ta Claus comes to - night.

I Wonder as I Wander

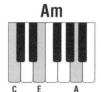 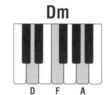 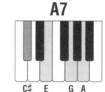 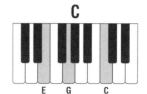

By John Jacob Niles

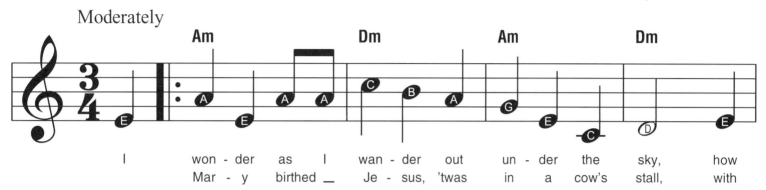

I won - der as I wan - der out un - der the sky, how
Mar - y birthed Je - sus, 'twas in a cow's stall, how with

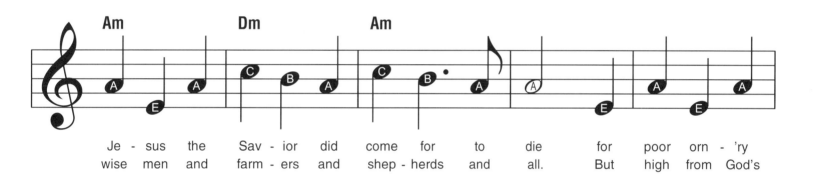

Je - sus the Sav - ior did come for to die. for poor orn - 'ry
wise men and farm - ers and shep - herds and all. But high from God's

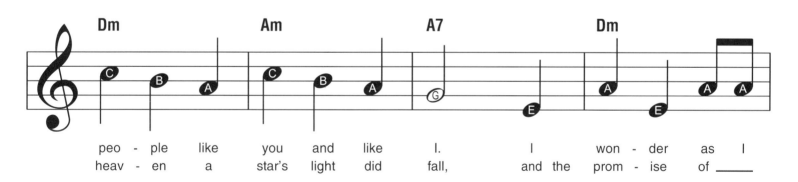

peo - ple like you and like I. I won - der as I
heav - en a star's light did fall, and the prom - ise of

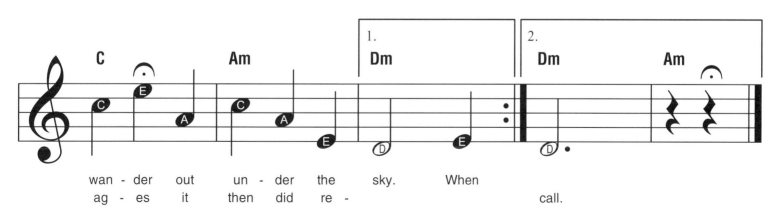

wan - der out un - der the sky. When
ag - es it then did re - call.

A Holly Jolly Christmas

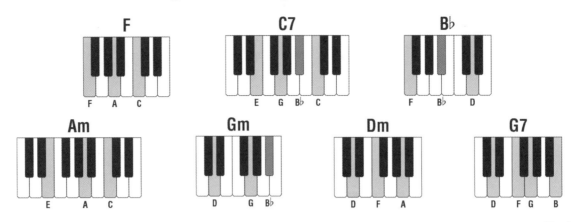

Music and Lyrics by
Johnny Marks

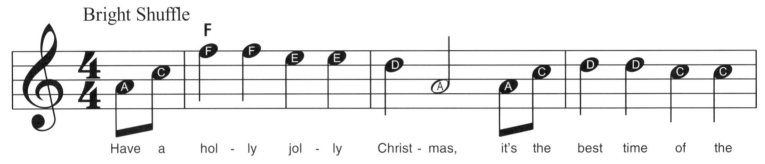

Have a hol - ly jol - ly Christ - mas, it's the best time of the

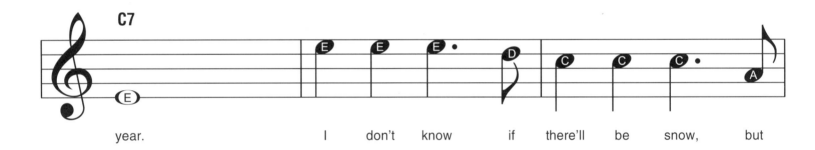

year. I don't know if there'll be snow, but

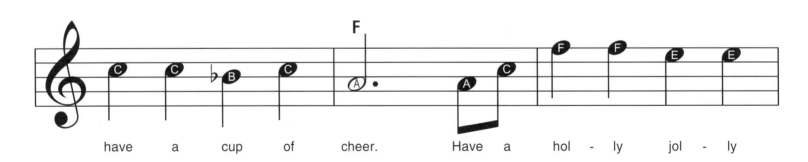

have a cup of cheer. Have a hol - ly jol - ly

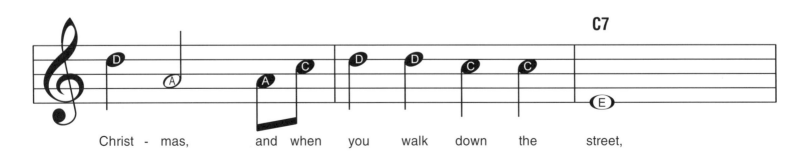

Christ - mas, and when you walk down the street,

(There's No Place Like)
Home for the Holidays

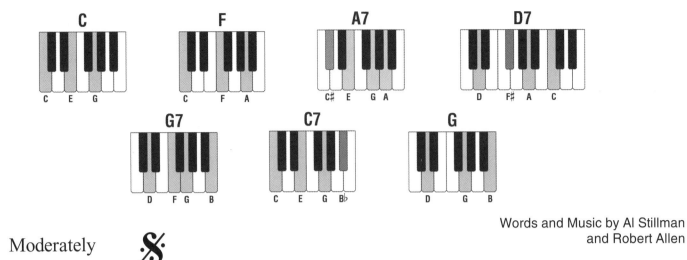

Words and Music by Al Stillman
and Robert Allen

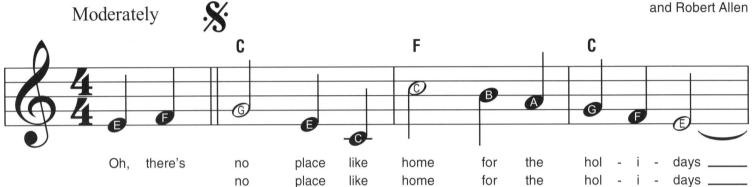

Oh, there's no place like home for the hol-i-days ____
no place like home for the hol-i-days ____

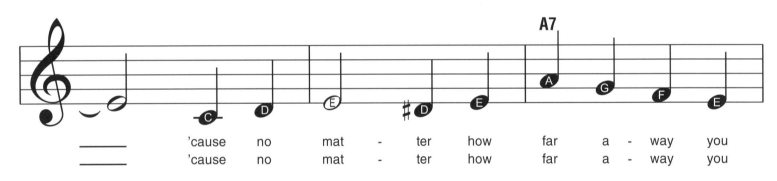

____ 'cause no mat-ter how far a-way you
____ 'cause no mat-ter how far a-way you

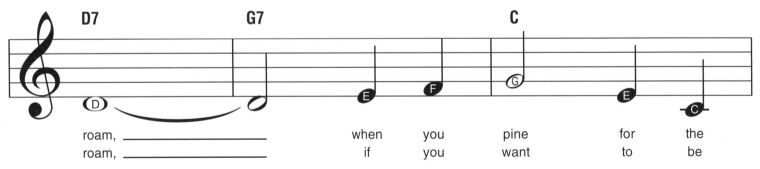

roam, ____ when you pine for the
roam, ____ if you pine want to be

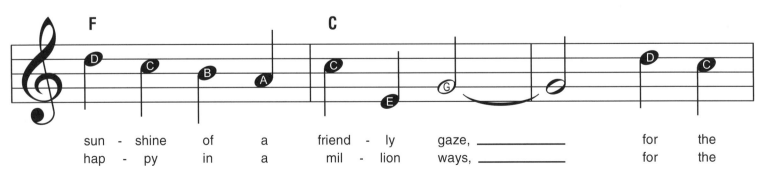

sun-shine of a friend-ly gaze, ____ for the
hap-py in a mil-lion ways, ____ for the

I Heard the Bells on Christmas Day

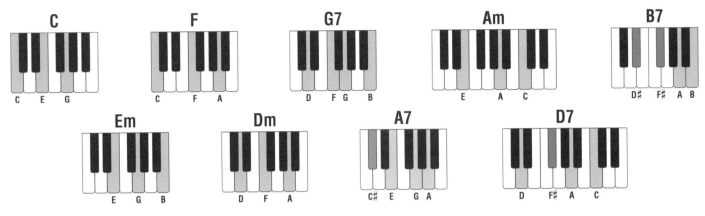

Words by Henry Wadsworth Longfellow
Adapted by Johnny Marks
Music by Johnny Marks

Moderately

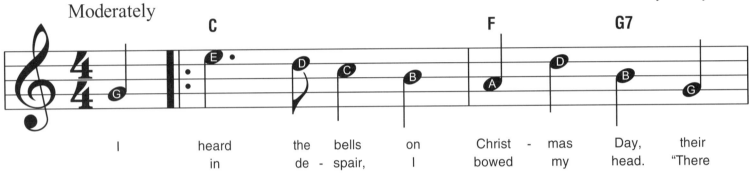

I heard the bells on Christ - mas Day, their
in de - spair, I bowed my head. "There

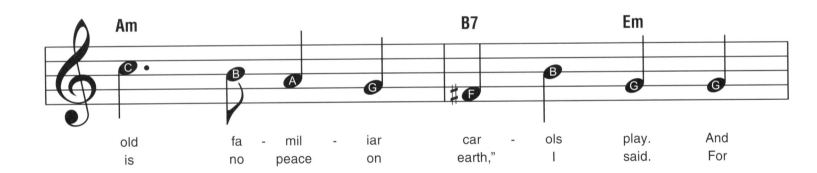

old fa - mil - iar car - ols play. And
is no peace on earth," I said. And For

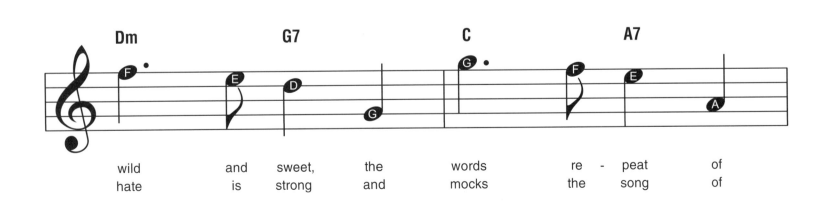

wild and sweet, the words re - peat of
hate is strong and mocks the song of

I Saw Mommy Kissing Santa Claus

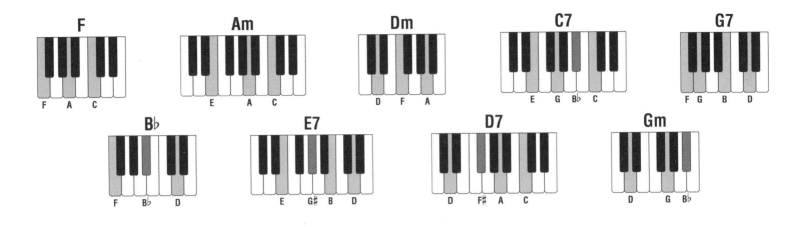

Words and Music by
Tommie Connor

Moderately

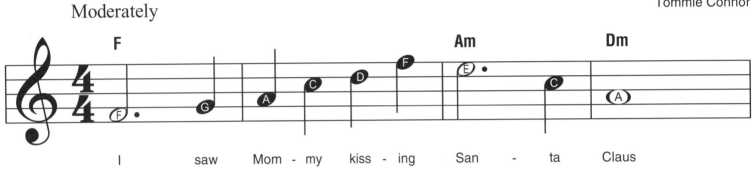

I saw Mom - my kiss - ing San - ta Claus

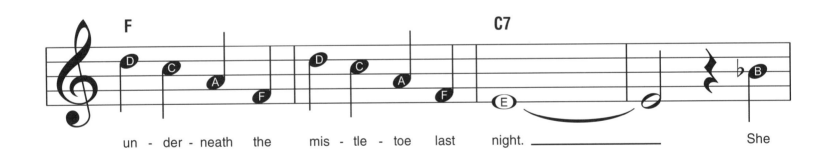

un - der - neath the mis - tle - toe last night. _____ She

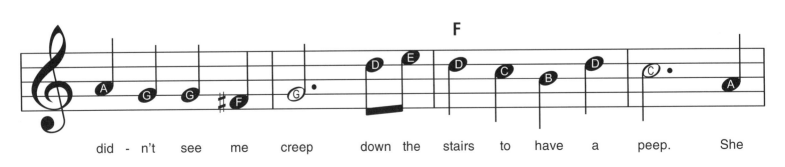

did - n't see me creep down the stairs to have a peep. She

61

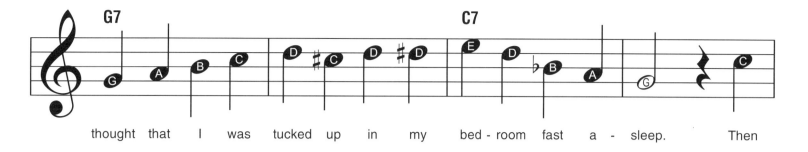

thought that I was tucked up in my bed-room fast a - sleep. Then

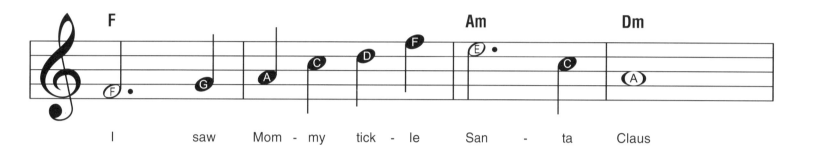

I saw Mom-my tick - le San - ta Claus

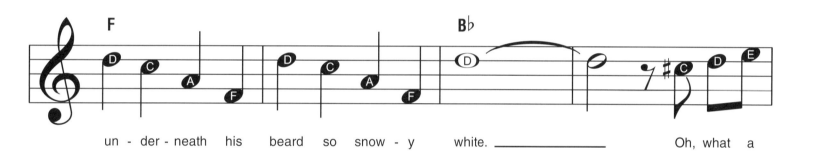

un - der-neath his beard so snow-y white. _____ Oh, what a

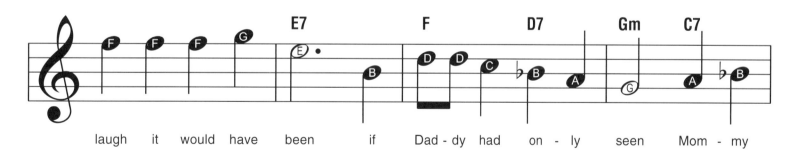

laugh it would have been if Dad-dy had on - ly seen Mom-my

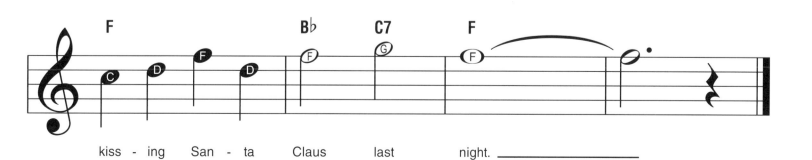

kiss - ing San - ta Claus last night. _____

I Want a Hippopotamus for Christmas

(Hippo the Hero)

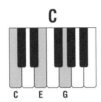
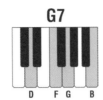
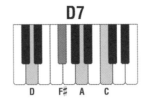
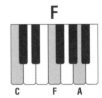

Words and Music by
John Rox

Brightly

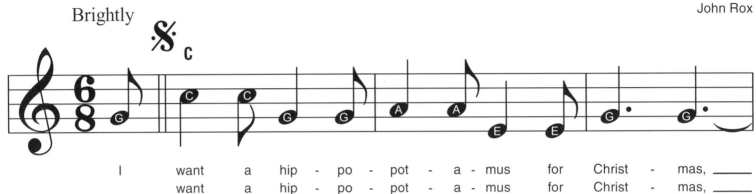

I want a hip - po - pot - a - mus for Christ - mas, _____
want a hip - po - pot - a - mus for Christ - mas, _____

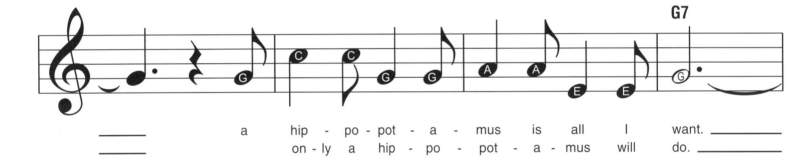

_____ a hip - po - pot - a - mus is all I want. _____
_____ on - ly a hip - po - pot - a - mus will do. _____

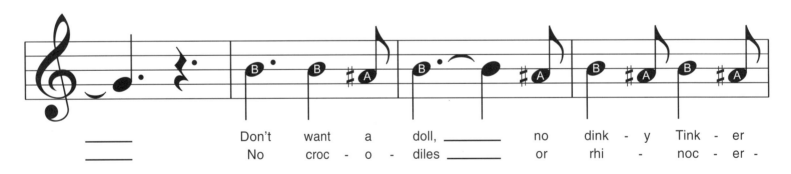

_____ Don't want a doll, _____ no dink - y Tink - er
_____ No croc - o - diles _____ or rhi - noc - er -

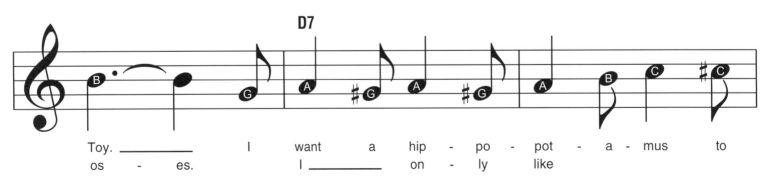

Toy. _____ I want a hip - po - pot - a - mus to
os - es. I _____ on - ly like

I'll Be Home for Christmas

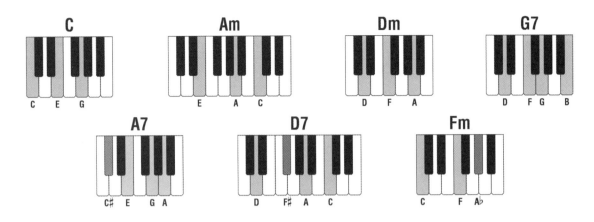

Words and Music by Kim Gannon
and Walter Kent

Moderately

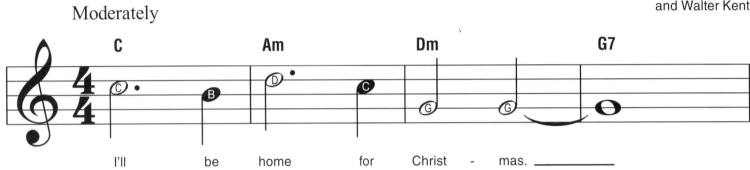

I'll be home for Christ - mas. _____

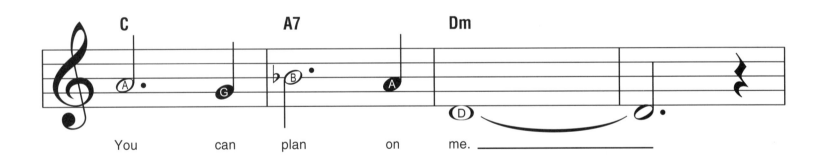

You can plan on me. _____

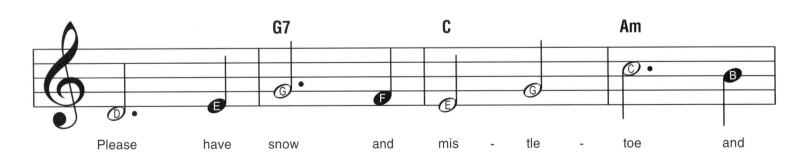

Please have snow and mis - tle - toe and

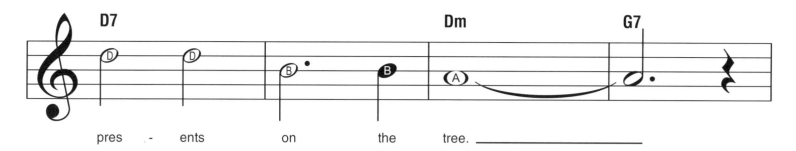

pres .- ents on the tree. _____

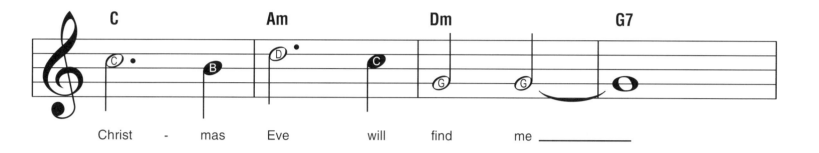

Christ - mas Eve will find me _____

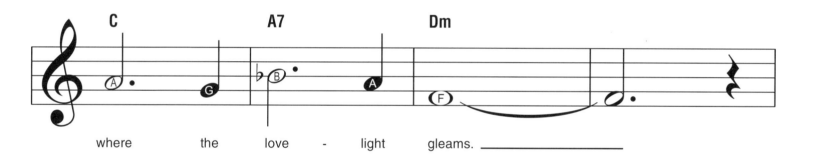

where the love - light gleams. _____

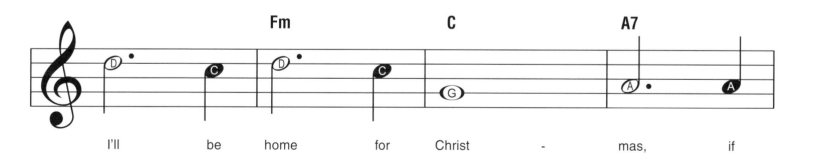

I'll be home for Christ - mas, if

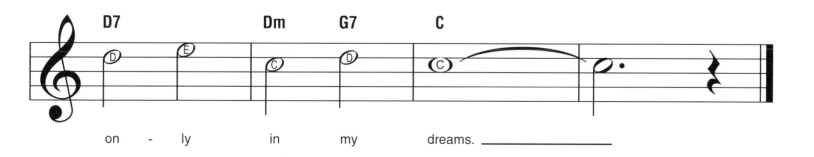

on - ly in my dreams. _____

It's Beginning to Look Like Christmas

By Meredith Willson

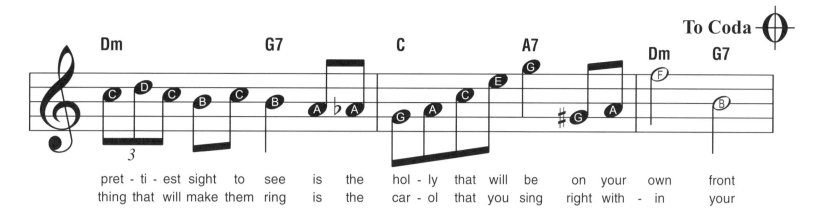

pret - ti - est sight to see is the hol - ly that will be on your own front
thing that will make them ring is the car - ol that you sing right with - in your

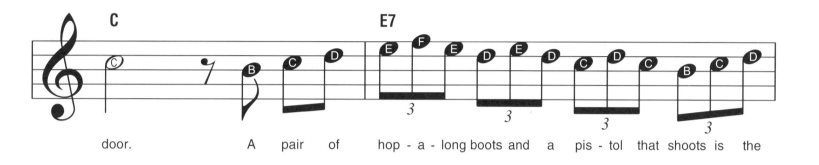

door. A pair of hop - a - long boots and a pis - tol that shoots is the

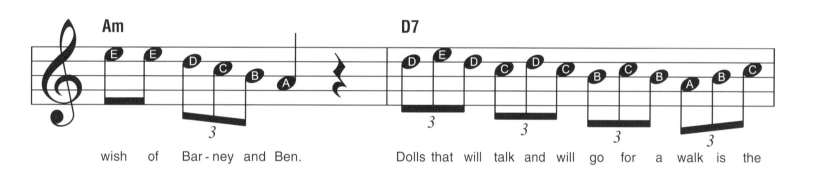

wish of Bar - ney and Ben. Dolls that will talk and will go for a walk is the

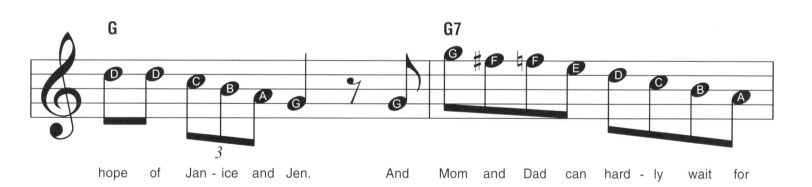

hope of Jan - ice and Jen. And Mom and Dad can hard - ly wait for

D.S. al Coda
(Return to 𝄋, play to ⊕
and skip to Coda)

CODA

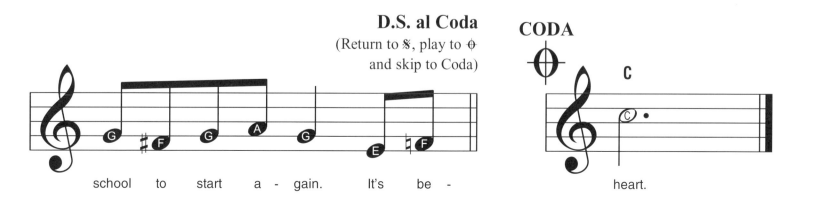

school to start a - gain. It's be -   heart.

Jingle Bell Rock

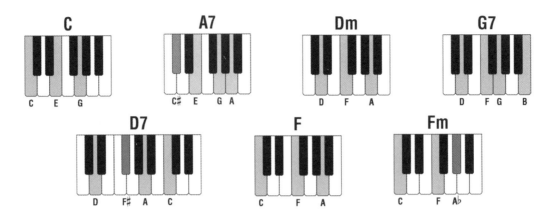

Words and Music by Joe Beal
and Jim Boothe

Moderately fast Shuffle

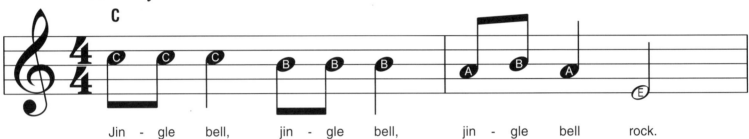

Jin - gle bell, jin - gle bell, jin - gle bell rock.

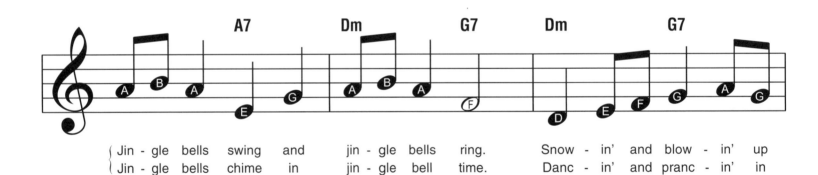

Jin - gle bells swing and jin - gle bells ring. Snow - in' and blow - in' up
Jin - gle bells chime in jin - gle bell time. Danc - in' and pranc - in' in

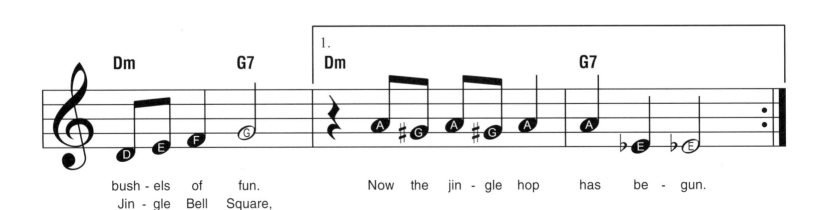

bush - els of fun. Now the jin - gle hop has be - gun.
Jin - gle Bell Square,

Last Christmas

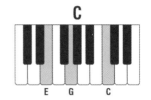
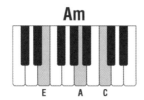
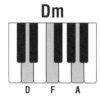

Words and Music by
George Michael

Moderately

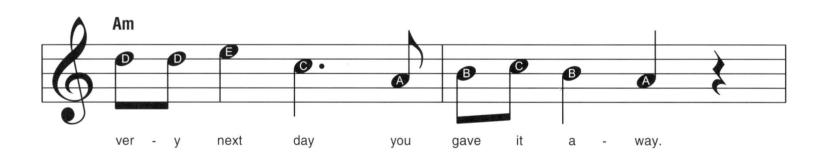

Last Christ - mas I gave you my heart, but the

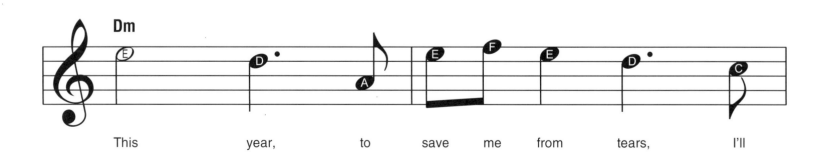

ver - y next day you gave it a - way.

This year, to save me from tears, I'll

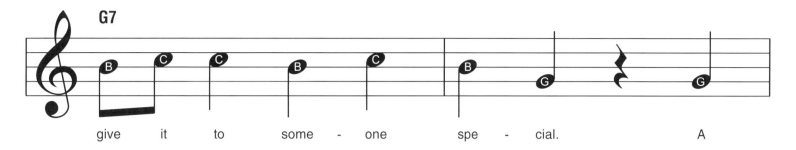

give it to some - one spe - cial. A

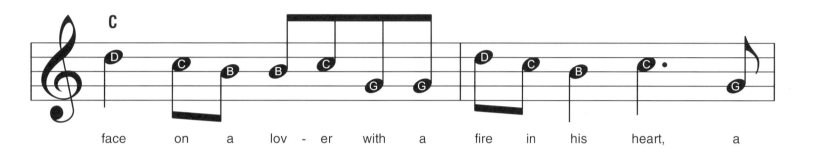

face on a lov - er with a fire in his heart, a

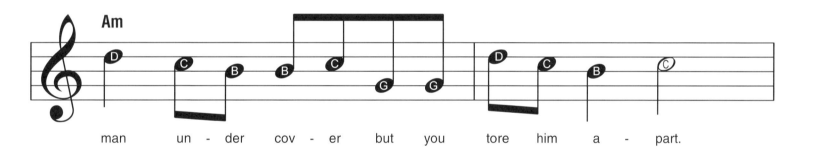

man un - der cov - er but you tore him a - part.

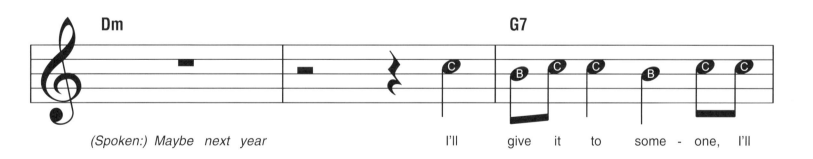

(Spoken:) Maybe next year I'll give it to some - one, I'll

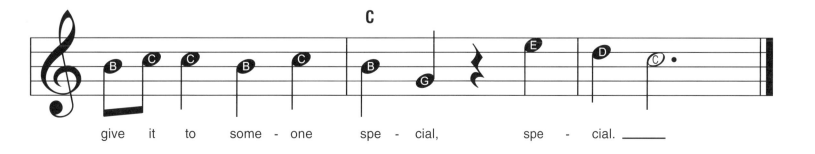

give it to some - one spe - cial, spe - cial. _____

Let It Snow!
Let It Snow! Let It Snow!

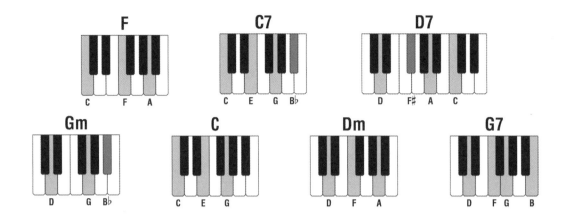

Words by Sammy Cahn
Music by Jule Styne

Oh, the weath-er out-side is fright-ful,
does-n't show signs of stop-ping,
but the
and I

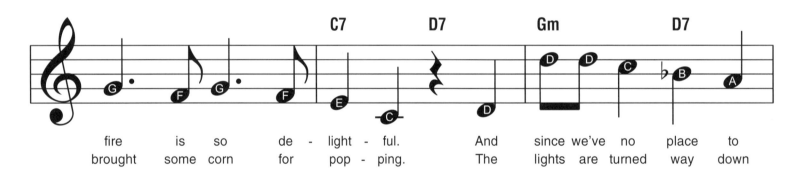

fire is so de-light-ful.
brought some corn for pop-ping.
And
The
since we've no place to
lights are turned way down

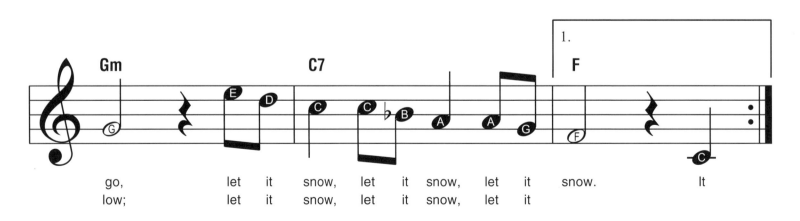

go,
low;
let it snow, let it snow, let it snow.
let it snow, let it snow, let it
It

The Little Drummer Boy

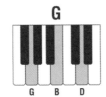
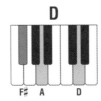

Words and Music by Harry Simeone,
Henry Onorati and Katherine Davis

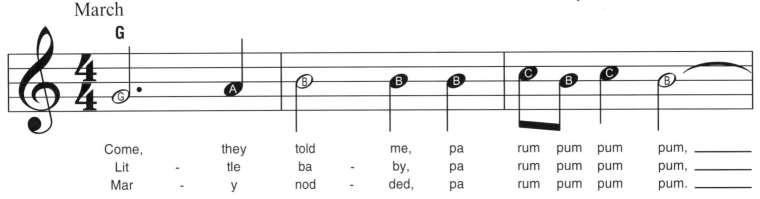

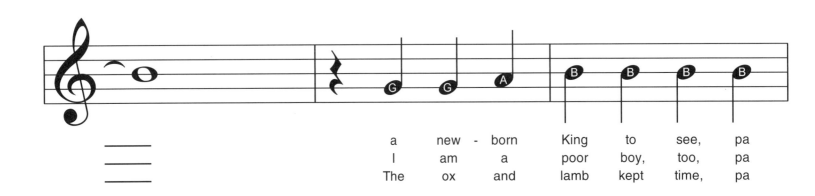

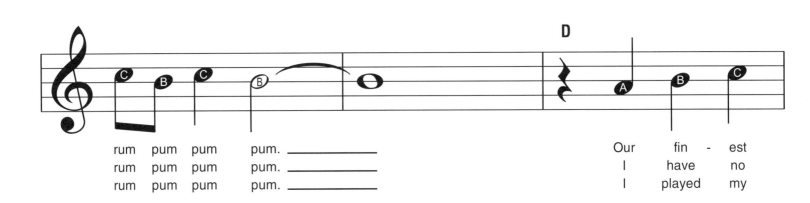

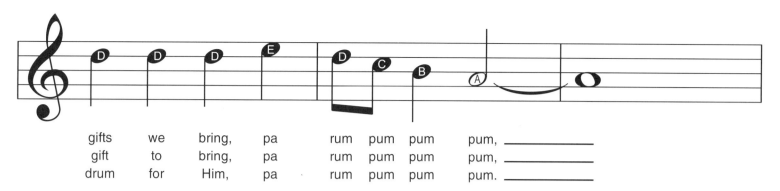

gifts	we	bring,	pa	rum	pum	pum	pum, _____
gift	to	bring,	pa	rum	pum	pum	pum, _____
drum	for	Him,	pa	rum	pum	pum	pum. _____

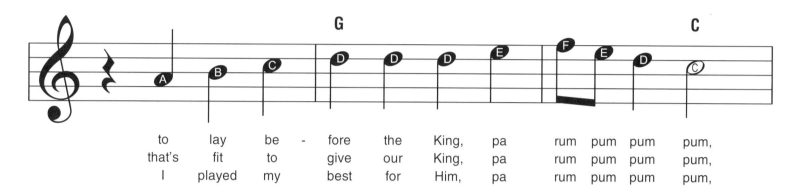

to	lay	be -	fore	the	King,	pa	rum	pum	pum	pum,
that's	fit	to	give	our	King,	pa	rum	pum	pum	pum,
I	played	my	best	for	Him,	pa	rum	pum	pum	pum,

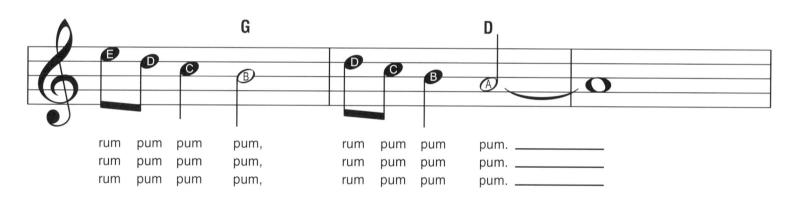

rum	pum	pum	pum,	rum	pum	pum	pum. _____
rum	pum	pum	pum,	rum	pum	pum	pum. _____
rum	pum	pum	pum,	rum	pum	pum	pum. _____

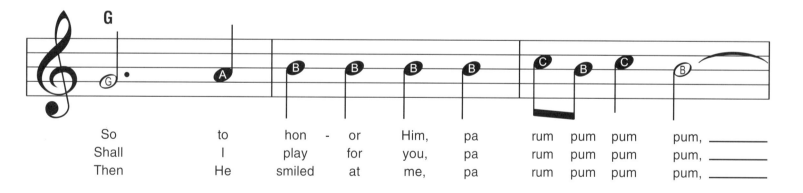

So	to	hon -	or	Him,	pa	rum	pum	pum	pum, _____
Shall	I	play	for	you,	pa	rum	pum	pum	pum, _____
Then	He	smiled	at	me,	pa	rum	pum	pum	pum, _____

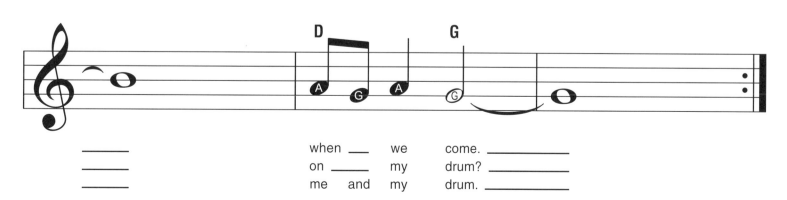

_____	when ___	we	come. _____
_____	on _____	my	drum? _____
_____	me	and	my	drum. _____

Little Saint Nick

Words and Music by Brian Wilson
and Mike Love

A Marshmallow World

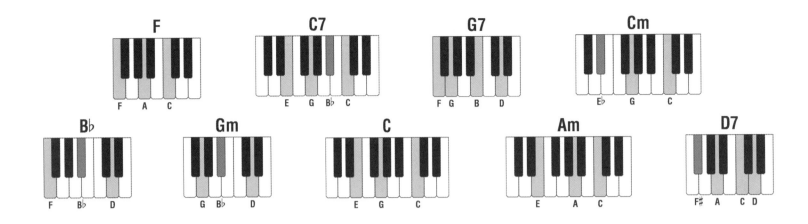

Words by Carl Sigman
Music by Peter De Rose

Moderate Shuffle

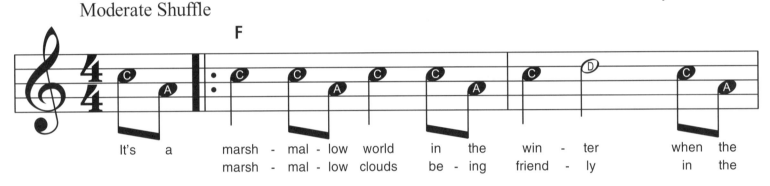

It's a marsh-mal-low world in the win-ter when the
marsh-mal-low clouds be-ing friend-ly in the

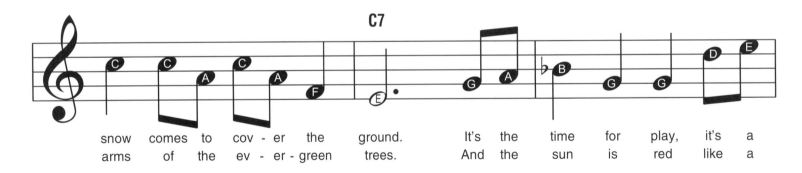

snow comes to cov-er the ground. It's the time for play, it's a
arms of the ev-er-green trees. And the sun is red like a

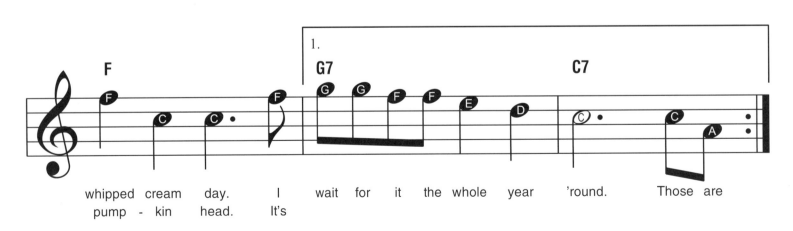

whipped cream day. I wait for it the whole year 'round. Those are
pump-kin head. It's

Mary, Did You Know?

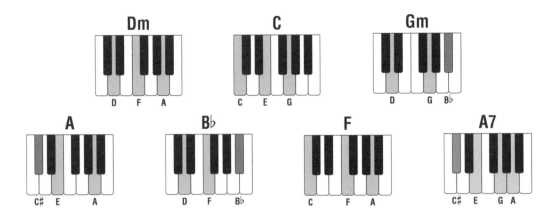

Words and Music by Mark Lowry
and Buddy Greene

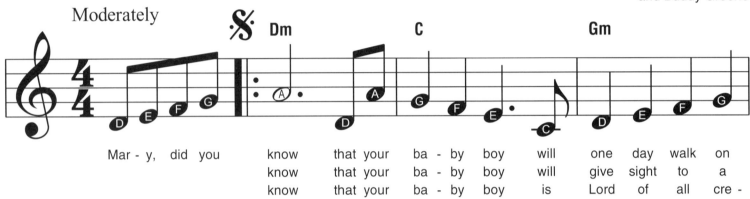

Mar - y, did you | know that your ba - by boy will | one day walk on
| know that your ba - by boy will | give sight to a
| know that your ba - by boy is | Lord of all cre -

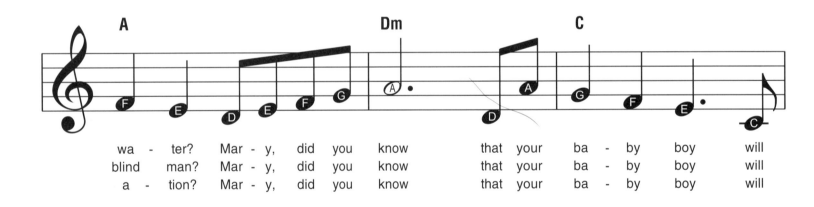

wa - ter? Mar - y, did you know | that your ba - by boy will
blind man? Mar - y, did you know | that your ba - by boy will
a - tion? Mar - y, did you know | that your ba - by boy will

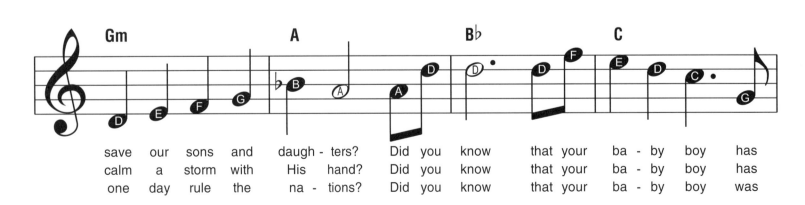

save our sons and | daugh - ters? Did you know | that your ba - by boy has
calm a storm with | His hand? Did you know | that your ba - by boy has
one day rule the | na - tions? Did you know | that your ba - by boy was

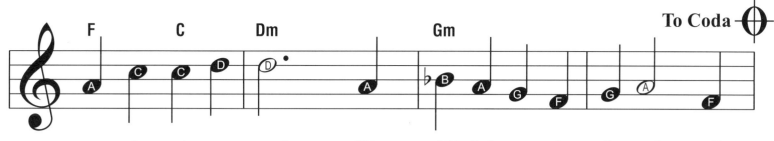

come to make you new? This child that you de - liv - ered will
walked where an - gels trod, and when you kiss your lit - tle ba - by, you've
heav - en's per - fect Lamb, and the sleep - ing child you're hold - ing is the

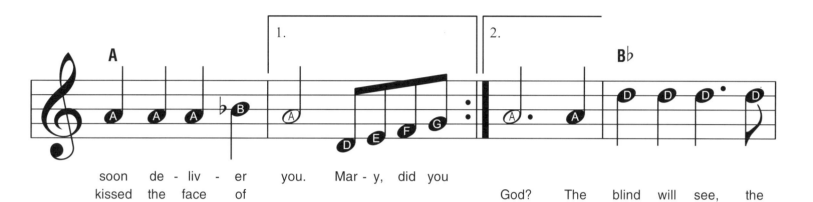

soon de - liv - er you. Mar - y, did you
kissed the face of God? The blind will see, the

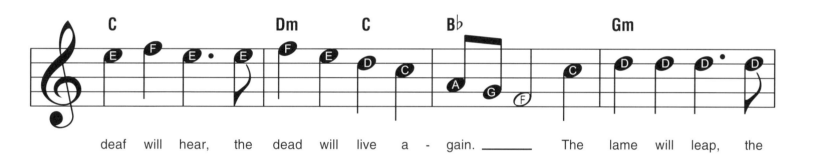

deaf will hear, the dead will live a - gain. _____ The lame will leap, the

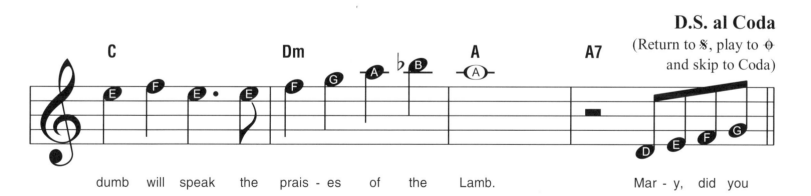

dumb will speak the prais - es of the Lamb. Mar - y, did you

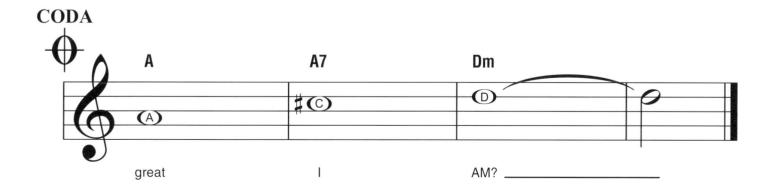

great I AM? _____

Merry Christmas, Darling

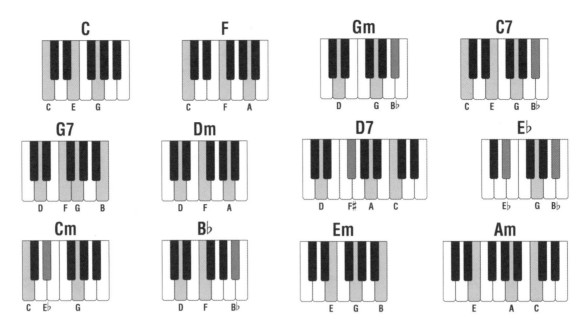

Words and Music by Richard Carpenter
and Frank Pooler

Moderately

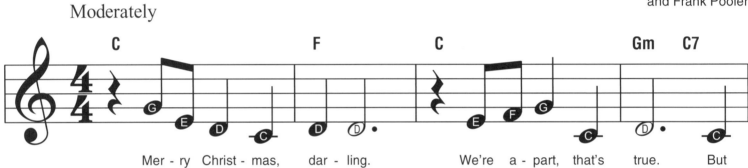

Mer - ry Christ - mas, dar - ling. We're a - part, that's true. But

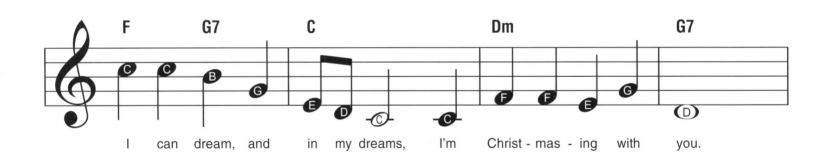

I can dream, and in my dreams, I'm Christ - mas - ing with you.

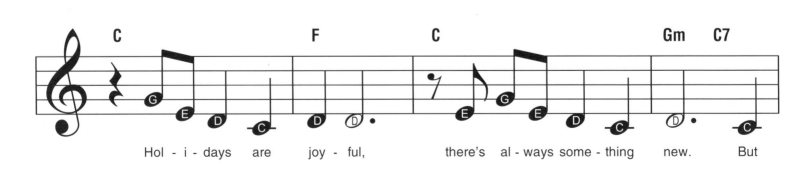

Hol - i - days are joy - ful, there's al - ways some - thing new. But

Mistletoe and Holly

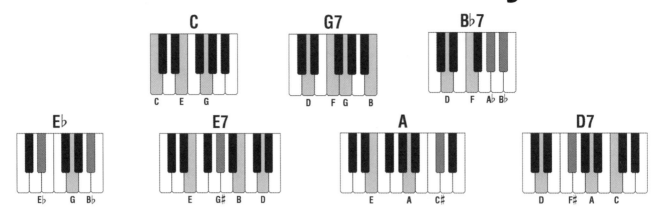

Words and Music by Frank Sinatra,
Dok Stanford and Henry W. Sanicola

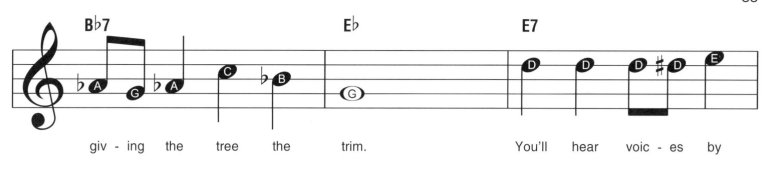

giv - ing the tree the trim. You'll hear voic - es by

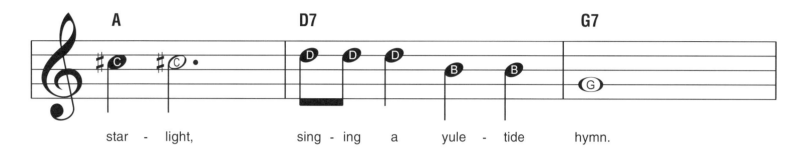

star - light, sing - ing a yule - tide hymn.

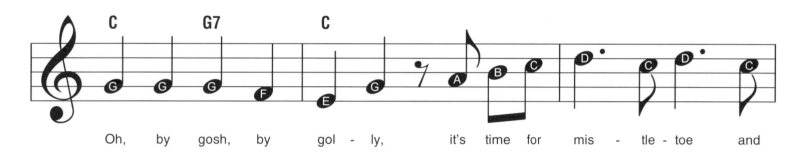

Oh, by gosh, by gol - ly, it's time for mis - tle - toe and

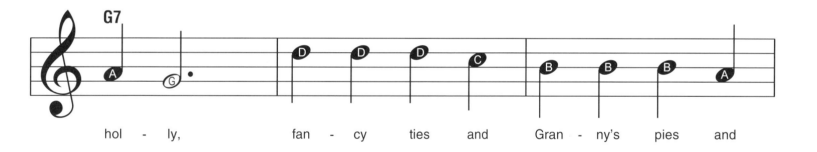

hol - ly, fan - cy ties and Gran - ny's pies and

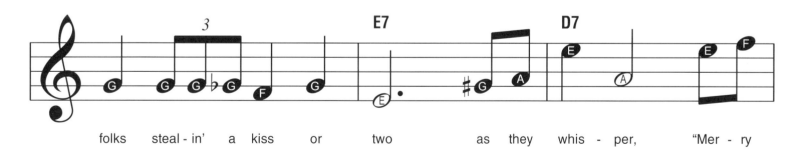

folks steal - in' a kiss or two as they whis - per, "Mer - ry

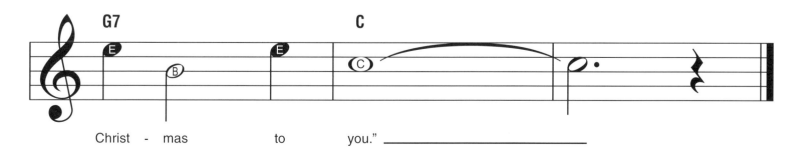

Christ - mas to you." _____

The Most Wonderful Time of the Year

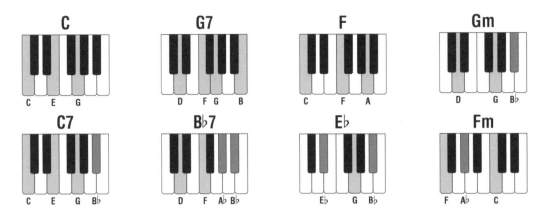

Words and Music by Eddie Pola
and George Wyle

Moderately, in 2

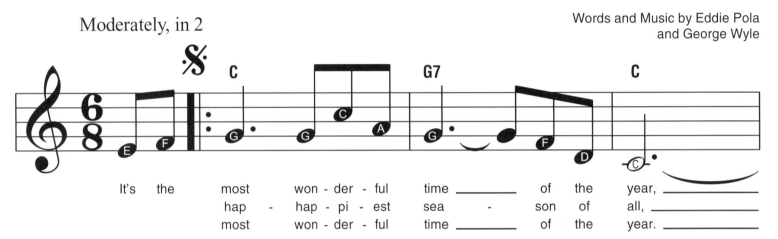

It's the most won-der-ful time _____ of the year, _____
hap - hap-pi-est sea - son of all, _____
most won-der-ful time _____ of the year. _____

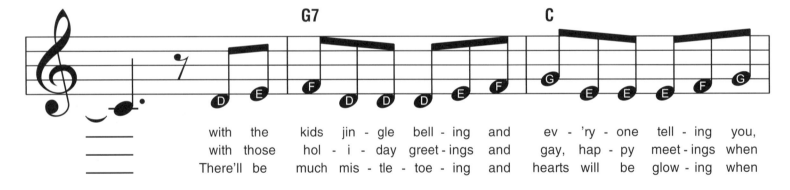

_____ with the kids jin-gle bell-ing and ev-'ry-one tell-ing you,
_____ with those hol-i-day greet-ings and gay, hap-py meet-ings when
_____ There'll be much mis-tle-toe-ing and hearts will be glow-ing when

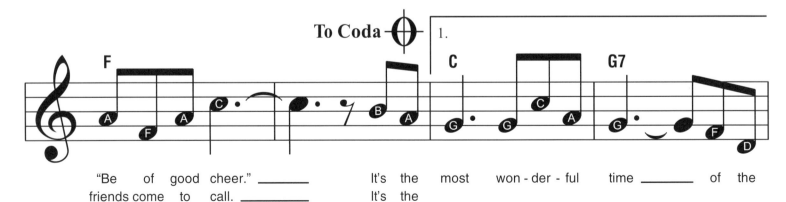

"Be of good cheer." _____ It's the most won-der-ful time _____ of the
friends come to call. _____ It's the
loved ones are near. _____ It's the

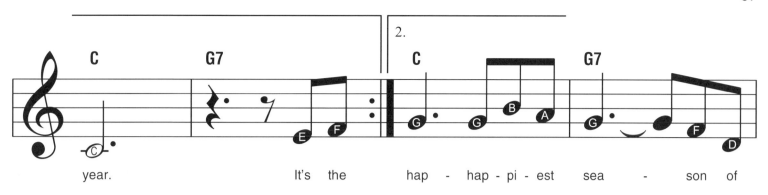

year. It's the hap - hap - pi - est sea - son of

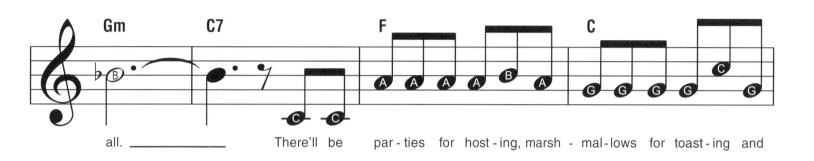

all. _____ There'll be par - ties for host - ing, marsh - mal - lows for toast - ing and

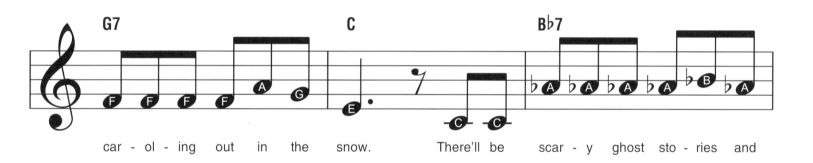

car - ol - ing out in the snow. There'll be scar - y ghost sto - ries and

D.S. al Coda
(Return to 𝄋, play to ⊕
and skip to Coda)

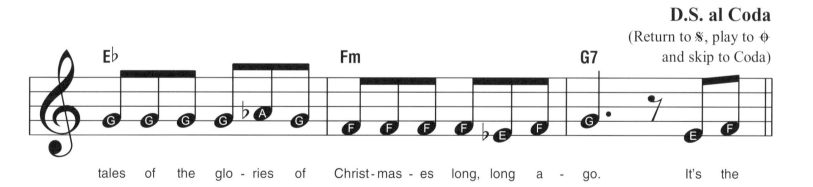

tales of the glo - ries of Christ - mas - es long, long a - go. It's the

CODA

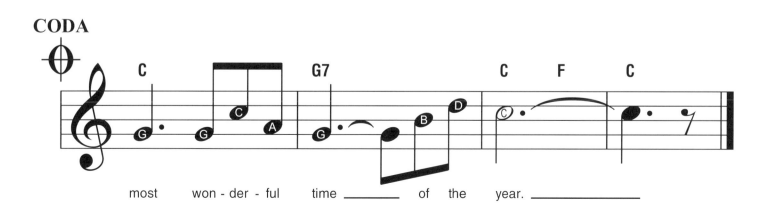

most won - der - ful time _____ of the year. _____

My Favorite Things

from THE SOUND OF MUSIC

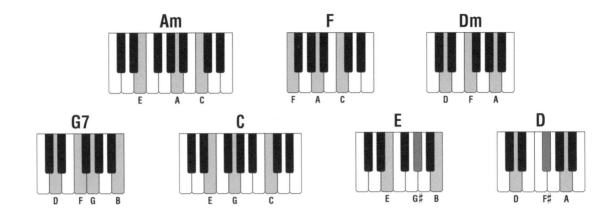

Lyrics by Oscar Hammerstein II
Music by Richard Rodgers

Moderately

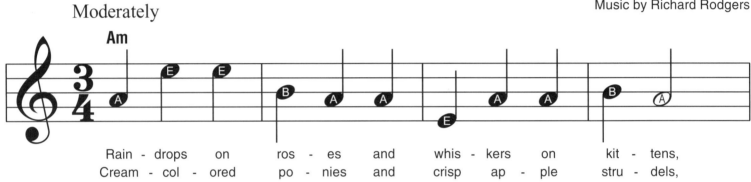

Rain - drops on ros - es and whis - kers on kit - tens,
Cream - col - ored po - nies and crisp ap - ple stru - dels,

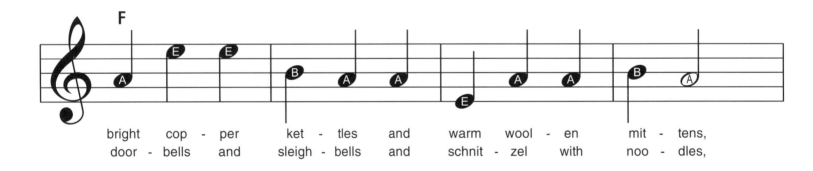

bright cop - per ket - tles and warm wool - en mit - tens,
door - bells and sleigh - bells and schnit - zel with noo - dles,

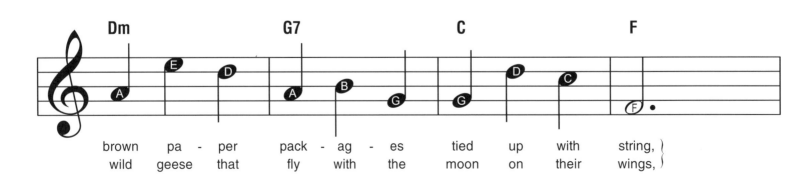

brown pa - per pack - ag - es tied up with string,
wild geese that fly with the moon on their wings,

Nuttin' for Christmas

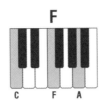
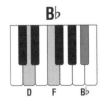
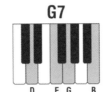
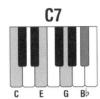
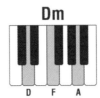

Words and Music by Roy C. Bennett
and Sid Tepper

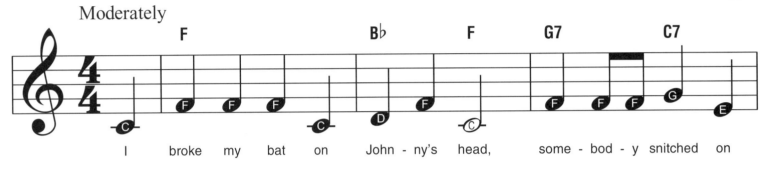

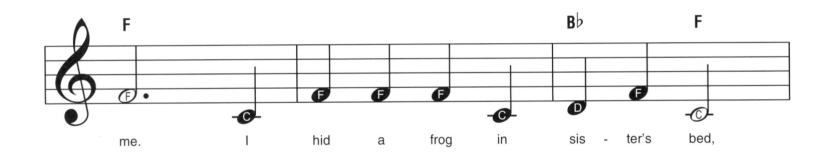

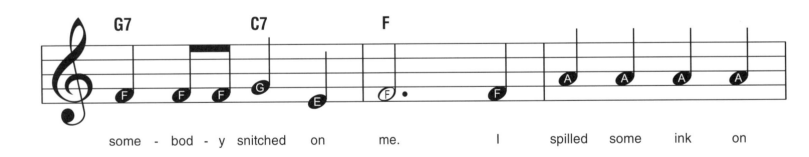

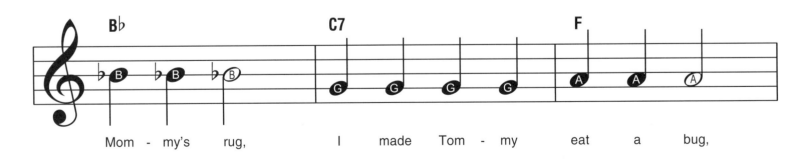

Pretty Paper

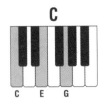
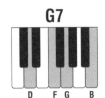

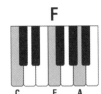
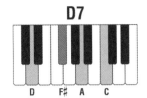

Words and Music by
Willie Nelson

Moderately

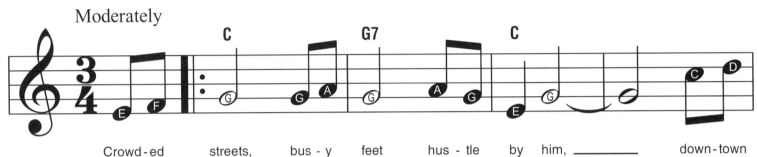

Crowd-ed streets, bus-y feet hus-tle by him, _____ down-town
stop? Bet-ter not, much too bus-y. You're in a

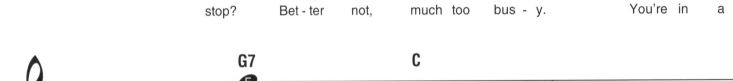

shop-pers, Christ-mas is nigh. _____ There he
hur-ry; my, how time does fly. _____ In the

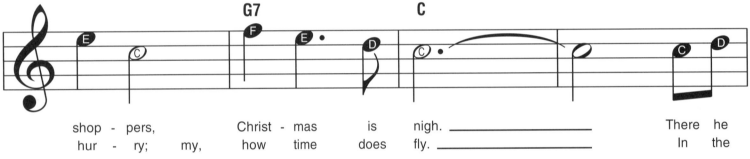

sits, all a-lone on the side-walk, _____
dis-tance the ring - ing of

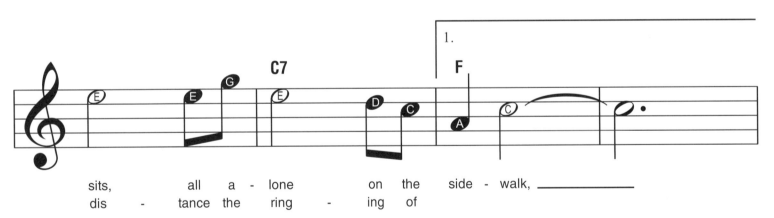

hop-ing that you won't pass him by. _____ Should you

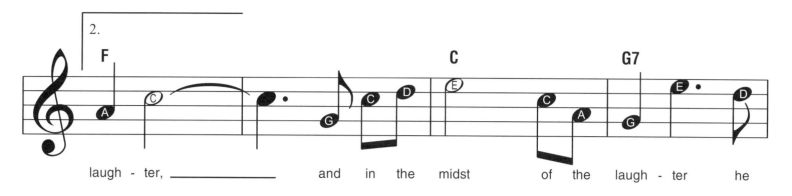

laugh - ter, _____ and in the midst of the laugh - ter he

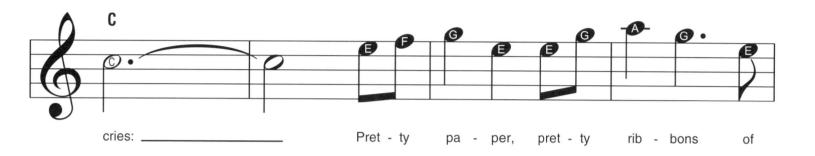

cries: _____ Pret - ty pa - per, pret - ty rib - bons of

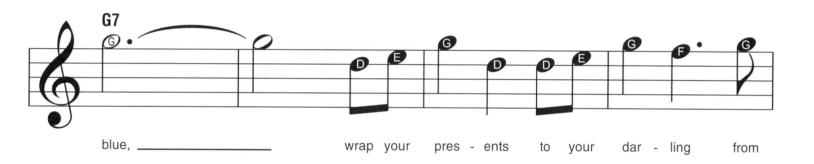

blue, _____ wrap your pres - ents to your dar - ling from

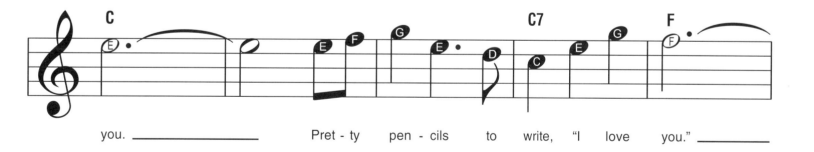

you. _____ Pret - ty pen - cils to write, "I love you." _____

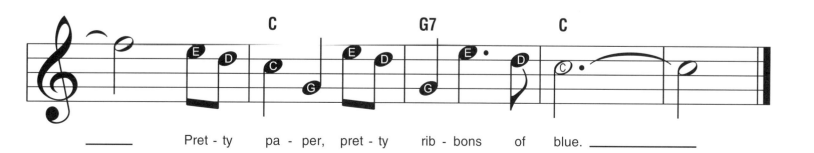

_____ Pret - ty pa - per, pret - ty rib - bons of blue. _____

Rockin' Around the Christmas Tree

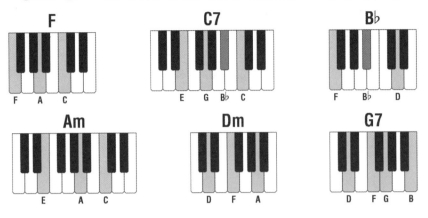

Music and Lyrics by
Johnny Marks

Bright Shuffle

Rock - in' a - round the Christ - mas tree at the Christ - mas par - ty
Rock - in' a - round the Christ - mas tree, let the Christ - mas spir - it

hop.   Mis - tle - toe hung where you can see, ev - 'ry
ring.   Lat - er we'll have where some pump - kin pie and we'll

1.   cou - ple tries to stop.

2.   do some car - ol -

ing.   You will get a sen - ti - men - tal

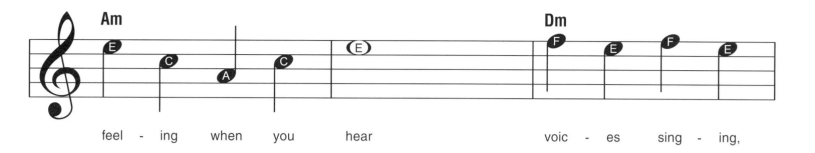

feel - ing when you hear voic - es sing - ing,

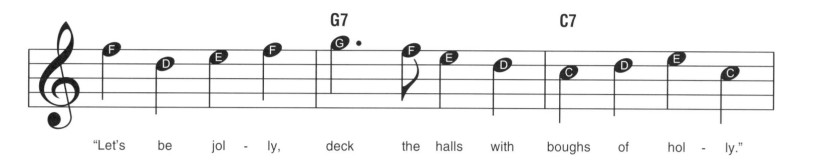

"Let's be jol - ly, deck the halls with boughs of hol - ly."

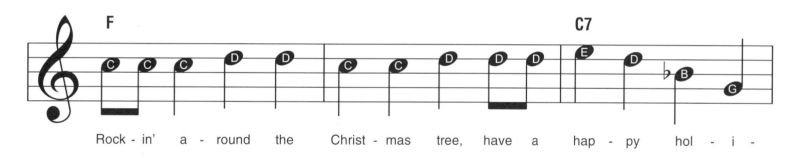

Rock - in' a - round the Christ - mas tree, have a hap - py hol - i -

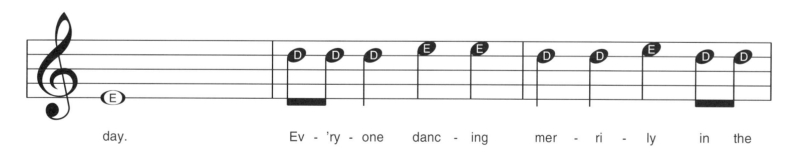

day. Ev - 'ry - one danc - ing mer - ri - ly in the

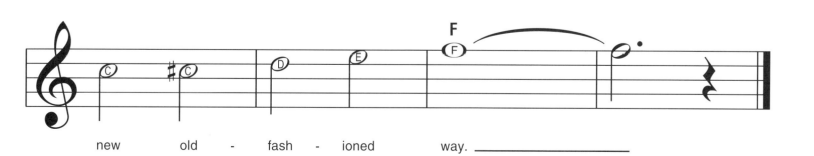

new old - fash - ioned way. _____

Rudolph the Red-Nosed Reindeer

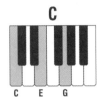
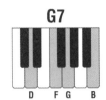
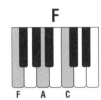
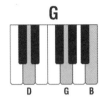
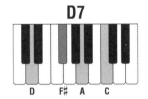

Music and Lyrics by
Johnny Marks

Bright Shuffle

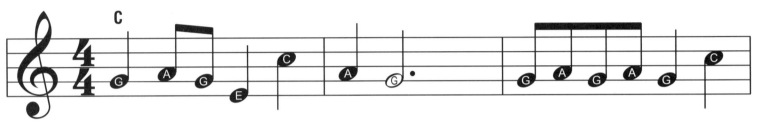

Ru - dolph the red - nosed rein - deer had a ver - y shin - y

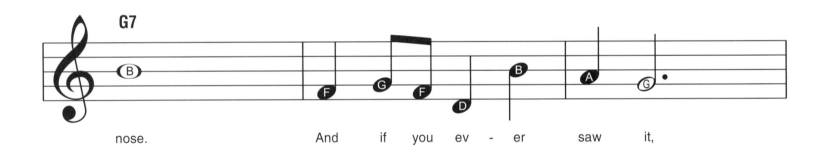

nose. And if you ev - er saw it,

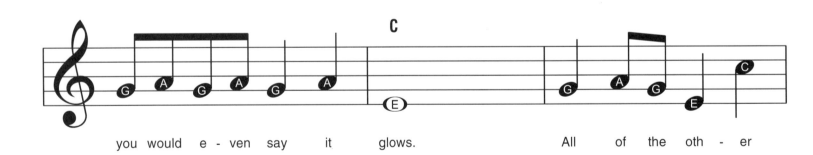

you would e - ven say it glows. All of the oth - er

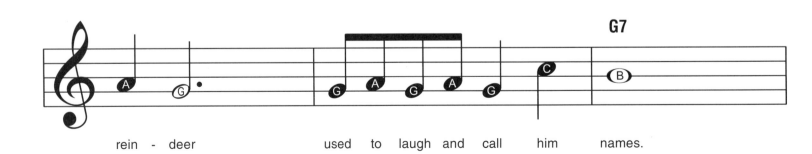

rein - deer used to laugh and call him names.

Santa Baby

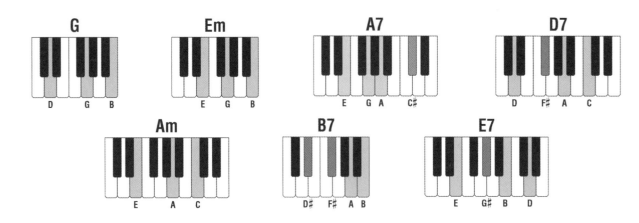

By Joan Javits,
Phil Springer and Tony Springer

Moderate Shuffle

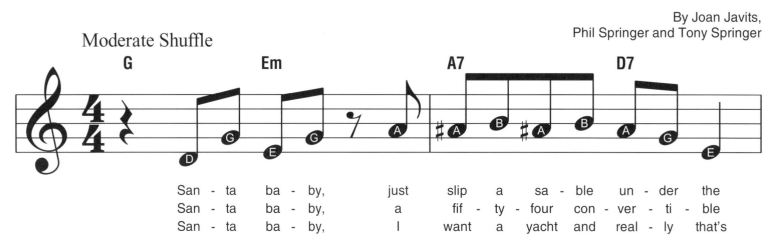

San - ta ba - by, just slip a sa - ble un - der the
San - ta ba - by, a fif - ty - four con - ver - ti - ble
San - ta ba - by, I want a yacht and real - ly that's

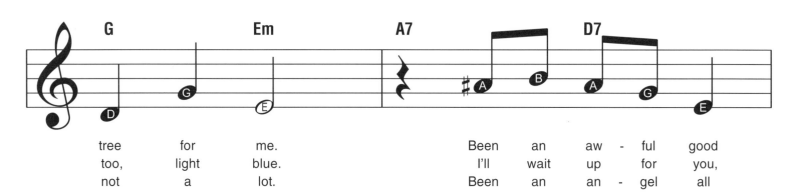

tree for me. Been an aw - ful good
too, light blue. I'll wait up for you,
not a lot. Been an an - gel all

To Coda ⊕

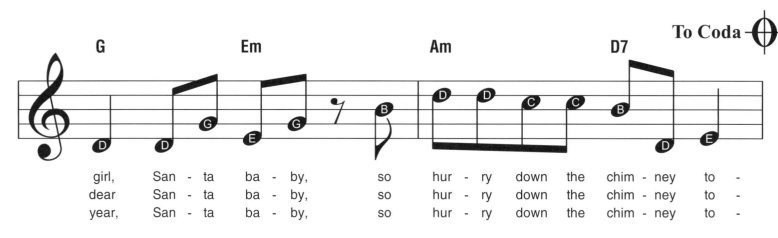

girl, San - ta ba - by, so hur - ry down the chim - ney to -
dear San - ta ba - by, so hur - ry down the chim - ney to -
year, San - ta ba - by, so hur - ry down the chim - ney to -

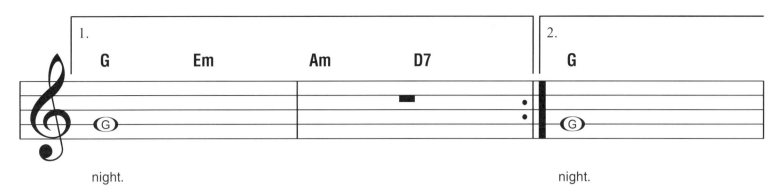

night.

night.

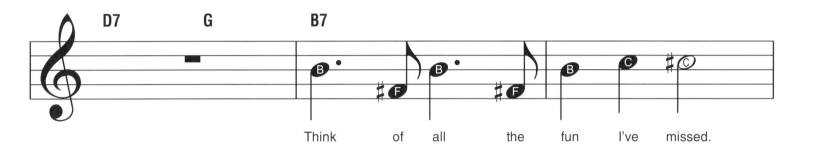

Think of all the fun I've missed.

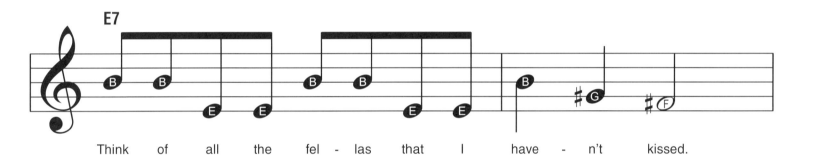

Think of all the fel - las that I have - n't kissed.

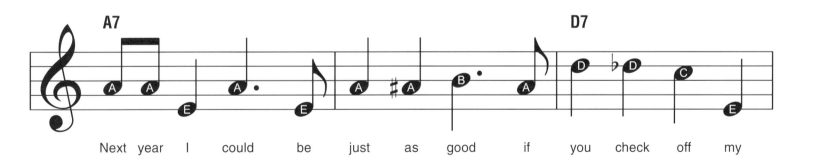

Next year I could be just as good if you check off my

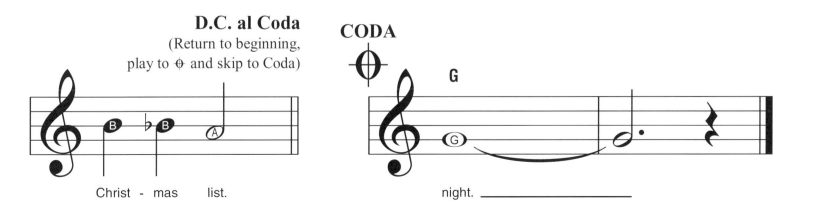

D.C. al Coda
(Return to beginning,
play to ⊕ and skip to Coda)

Christ - mas list.

CODA

night. _____

Santa Claus Is Comin' to Town

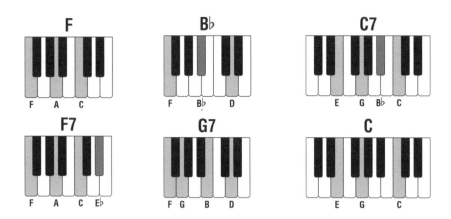

Words by Haven Gillespie
Music by J. Fred Coots

Bright Shuffle

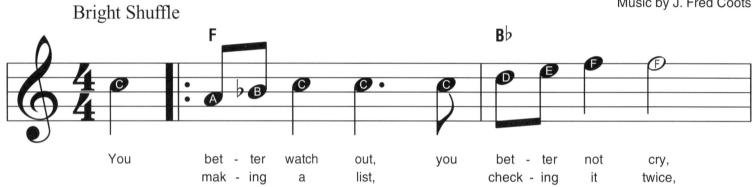

You — bet - ter watch out, you bet - ter not cry,
mak - ing a list, check - ing it twice,

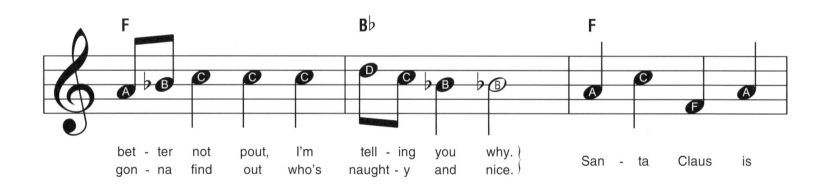

bet - ter not pout, I'm tell - ing you why. ⎫ San - ta Claus is
gon - na find out who's naught - y and nice. ⎭

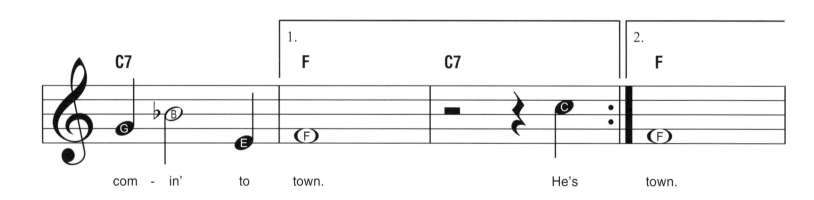

com - in' to town.   He's   town.

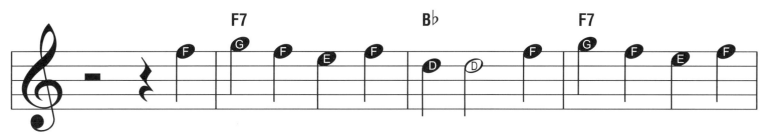

He sees you when you're sleep - ing, he knows when you're a -

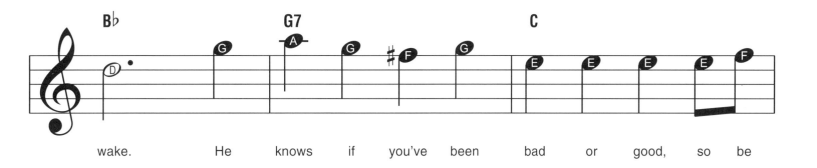

wake. He knows if you've been bad or good, so be

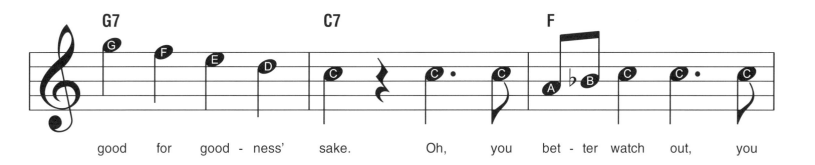

good for good - ness' sake. Oh, you bet - ter watch out, you

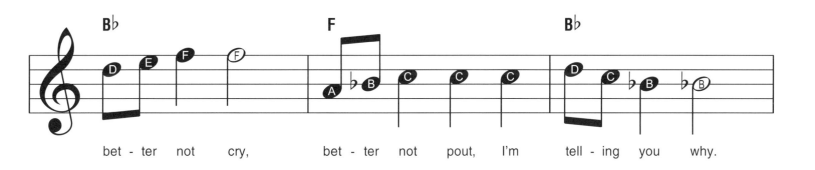

bet - ter not cry, bet - ter not pout, I'm tell - ing you why.

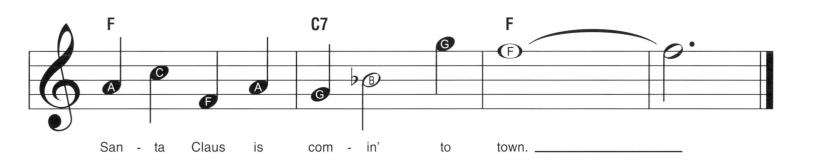

San - ta Claus is com - in' to town. _____

Silver and Gold

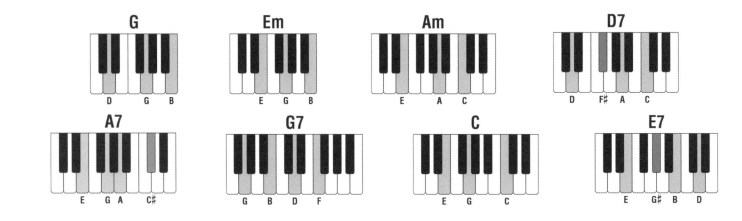

Music and Lyrics by
Johnny Marks

Moderate Waltz

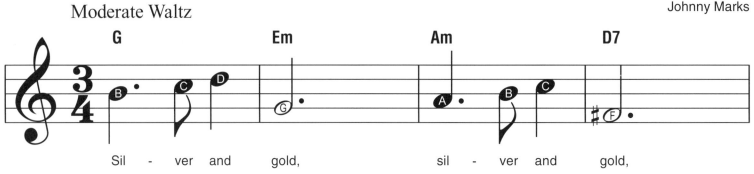

Sil - ver and gold, sil - ver and gold,

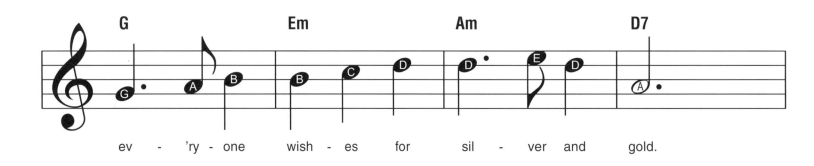

ev - 'ry - one wish - es for sil - ver and gold.

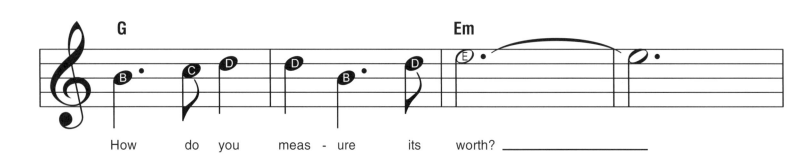

How do you meas - ure its worth? _____

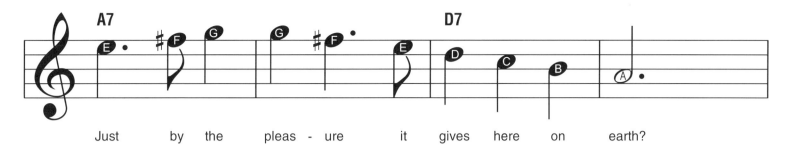

Just by the pleas - ure it gives here on earth?

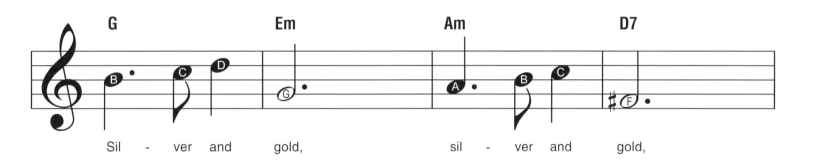

Sil - ver and gold, sil - ver and gold,

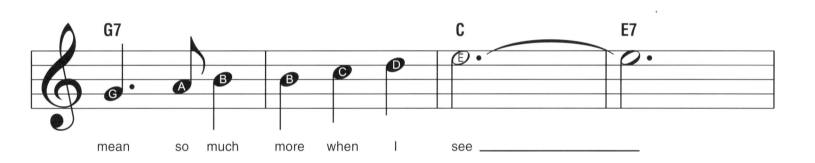

mean so much more when I see _____

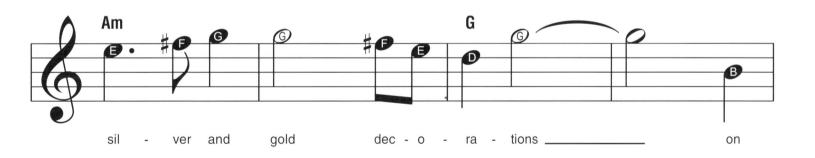

sil - ver and gold dec - o - ra - tions _____ on

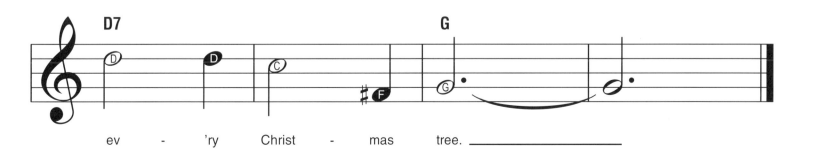

ev - 'ry Christ - mas tree. _____

Silver Bells
from the Paramount Picture THE LEMON DROP KID

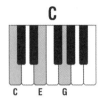 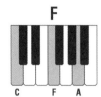 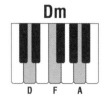 

Words and Music by Jay Livingston
and Ray Evans

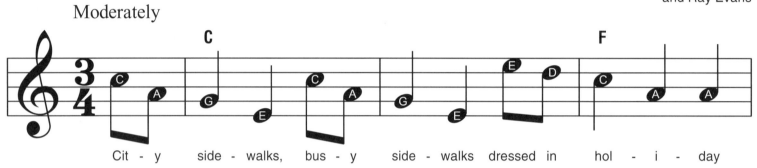

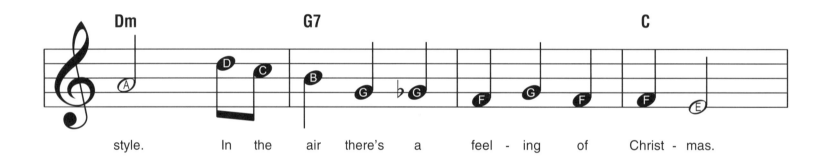

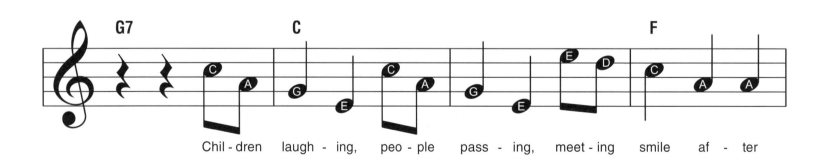

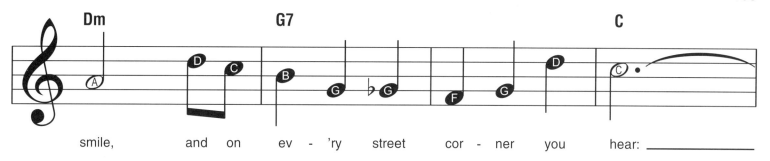

smile, and on ev - 'ry street cor - ner you hear: _____

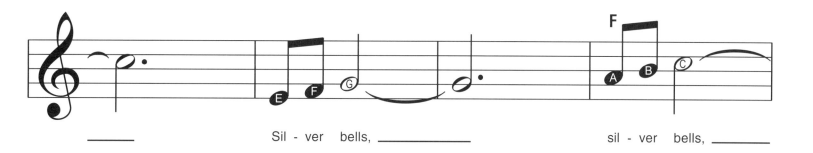

_____ Sil - ver bells, _____ sil - ver bells, _____

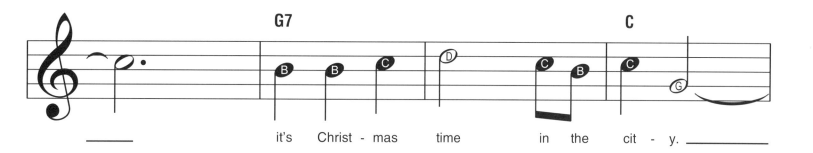

_____ it's Christ - mas time in the cit - y. _____

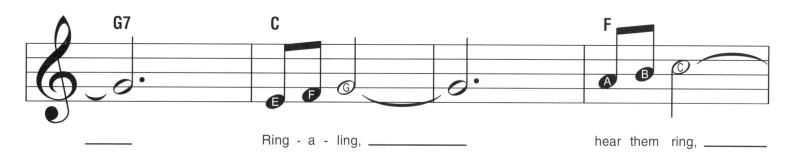

_____ Ring - a - ling, _____ hear them ring, _____

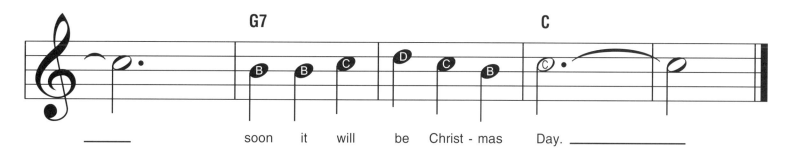

_____ soon it will be Christ - mas Day. _____

Sleigh Ride

Music by Leroy Anderson
Words by Mitchell Parish

Somewhere in My Memory
from the Twentieth Century Fox Motion Picture HOME ALONE

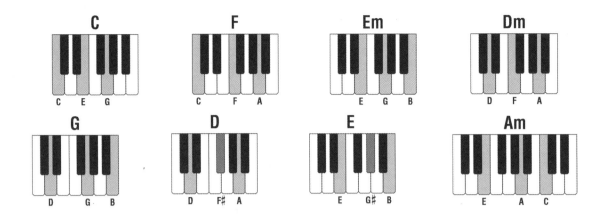

Words by Leslie Bricusse
Music by John Williams

Gently

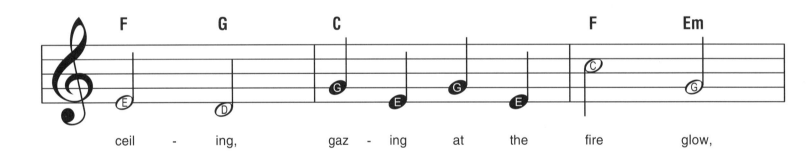

Can - dles in the win - dow, shad - ows paint - ing the

ceil - ing, gaz - ing at the fire glow,

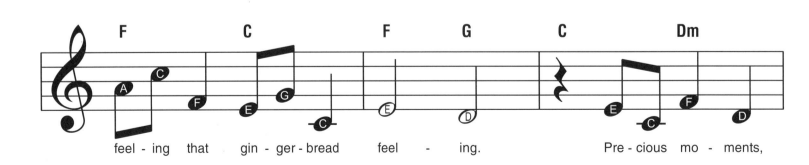

feel - ing that gin - ger - bread feel - ing. Pre - cious mo - ments,

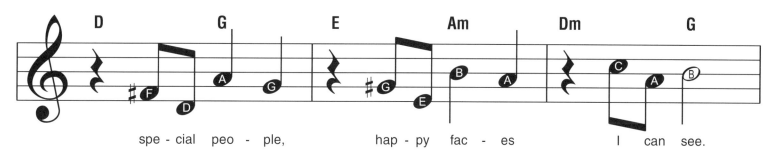

spe - cial peo - ple, hap - py fac - es I can see.

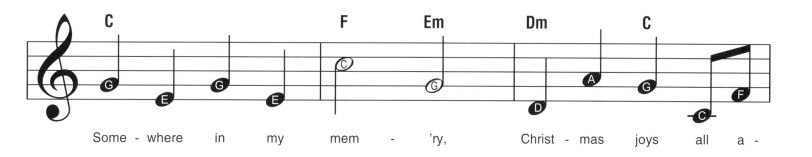

Some - where in my mem - 'ry, Christ - mas joys all a -

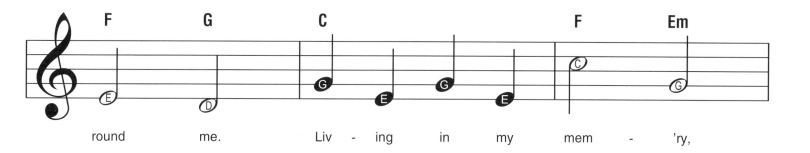

round me. Liv - ing in my mem - 'ry,

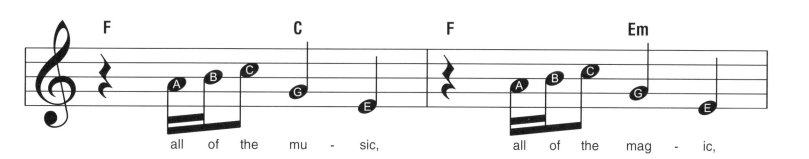

all of the mu - sic, all of the mag - ic,

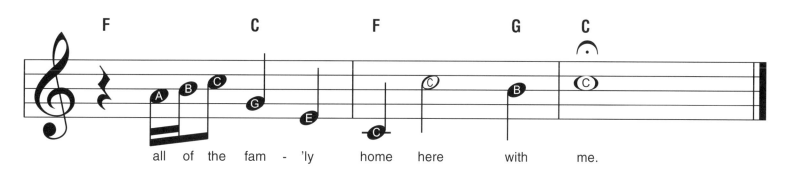

all of the fam - 'ly home here with me.

This Christmas

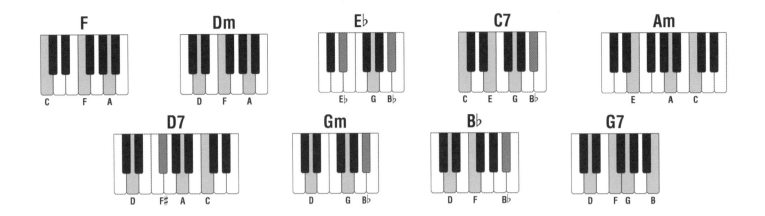

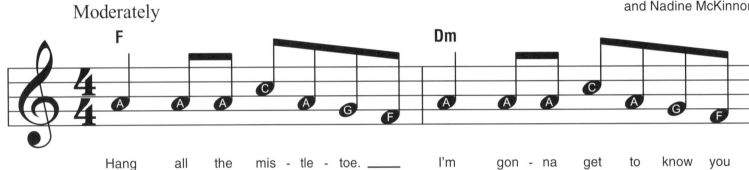

Words and Music by Donny Hathaway
and Nadine McKinnor

Moderately

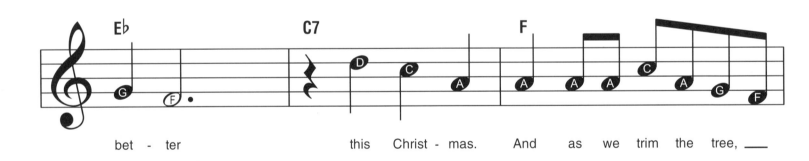

Hang all the mis - tle - toe. ____ I'm gon - na get to know you

bet - ter this Christ - mas. And as we trim the tree, ____

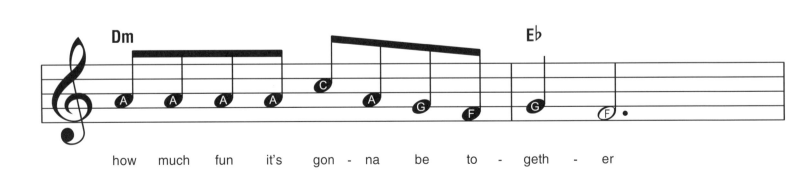

how much fun it's gon - na be to - geth - er

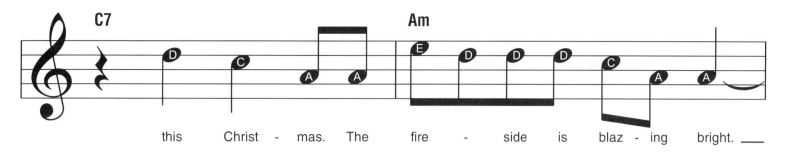

this Christ - mas. The fire - side is blaz - ing bright. _____

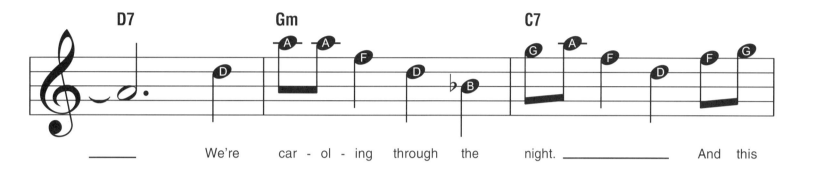

_____ We're car - ol - ing through the night. _____ And this

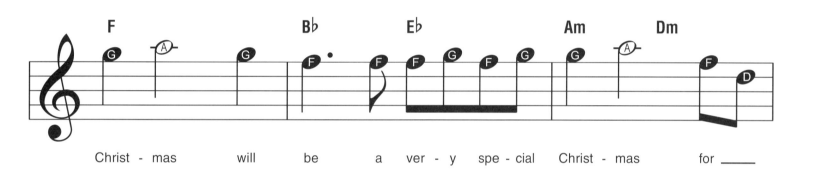

Christ - mas will be a ver - y spe - cial Christ - mas for _____

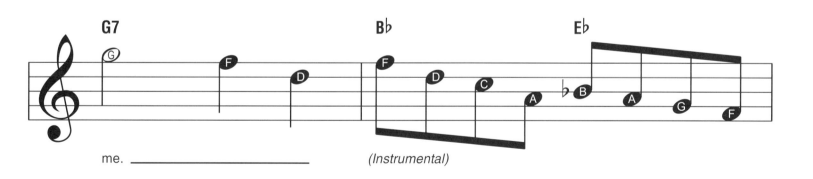

me. _____ (Instrumental)

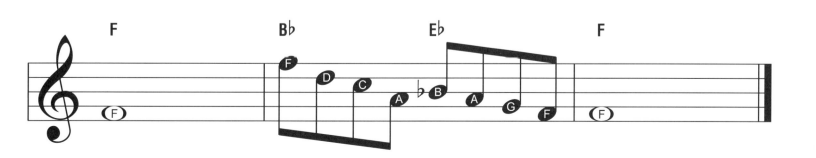

We Need a Little Christmas

from MAME

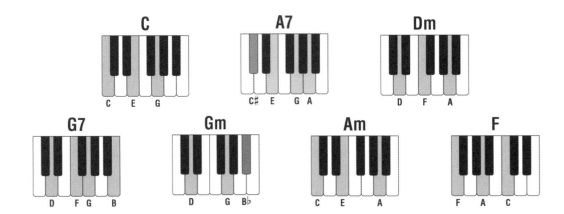

Music and Lyric by
Jerry Herman

Bright half-time feel

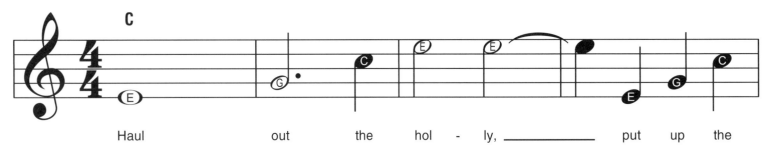

Haul out the hol - ly, _____ put up the

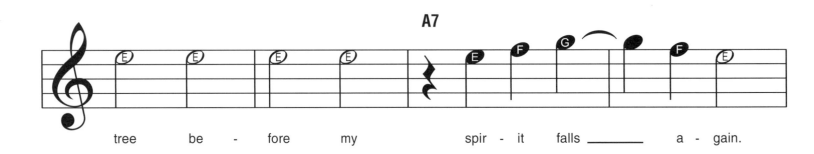

tree be - fore my spir - it falls _____ a - gain.

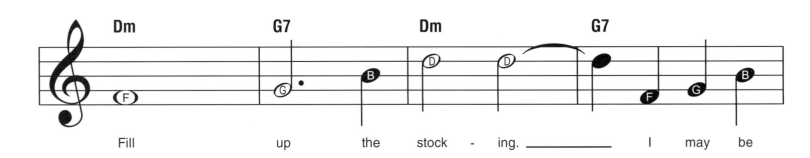

Fill up the stock - ing. _____ I may be

White Christmas

from the Motion Picture Irving Berlin's HOLIDAY INN

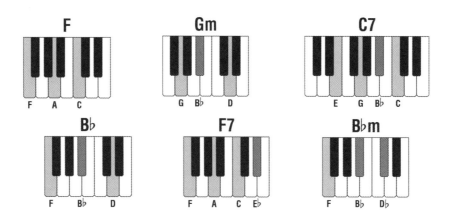

Words and Music by
Irving Berlin

Moderately

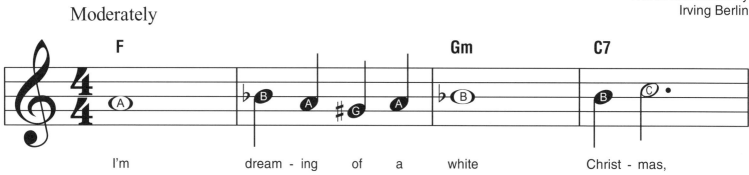

I'm   dream - ing   of   a   white   Christ - mas,

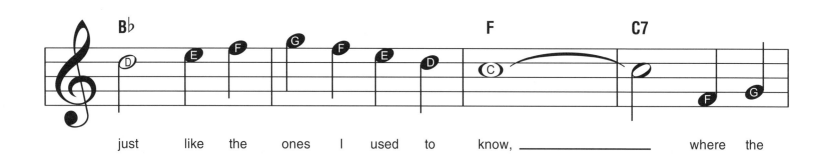

just   like   the   ones   I   used   to   know, _____ where the

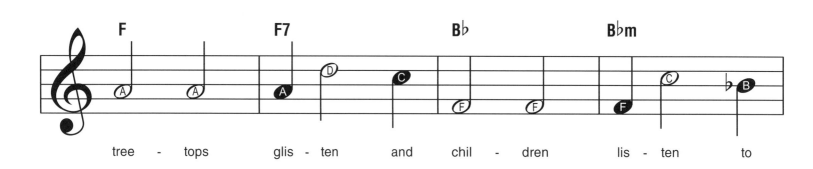

tree - tops   glis - ten   and   chil - dren   lis - ten   to   the

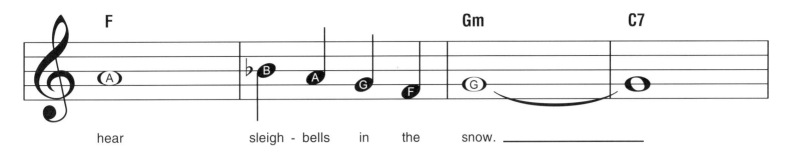

hear   sleigh - bells   in   the   snow. _____

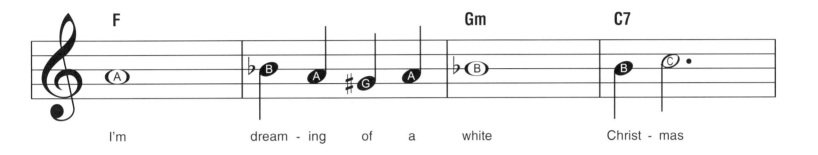

I'm   dream - ing   of   a   white   Christ - mas

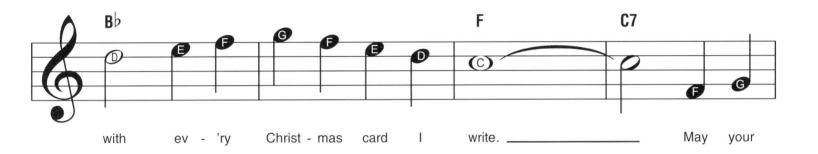

with   ev - 'ry   Christ - mas   card   I   write. _____   May   your

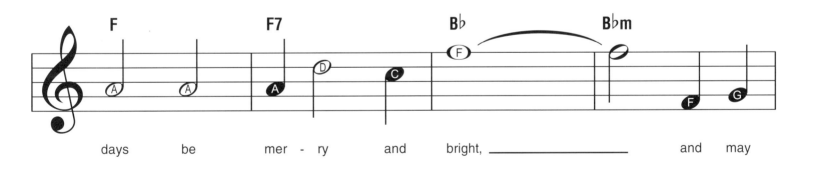

days   be   mer - ry   and   bright, _____   and   may

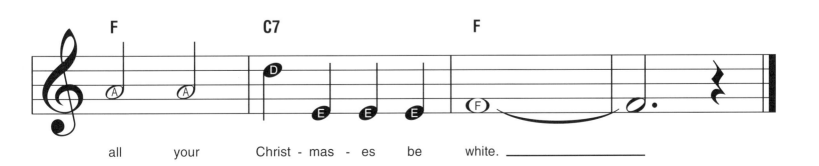

all   your   Christ - mas - es   be   white. _____

Winter Wonderland

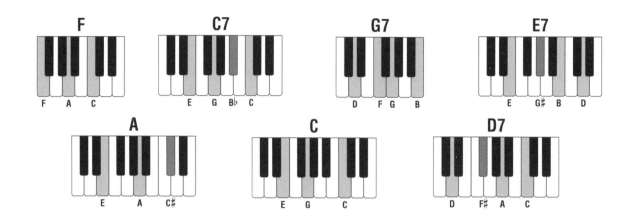

Words by Dick Smith
Music by Felix Bernard

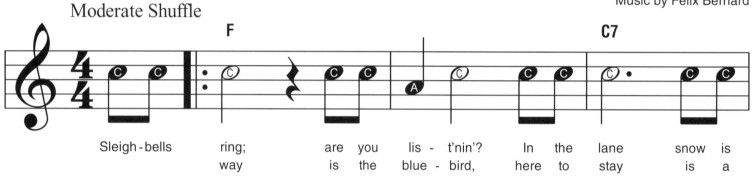

Sleigh-bells ring; are you lis - t'nin'? In the lane snow is
way is the blue - bird, here to stay snow is a

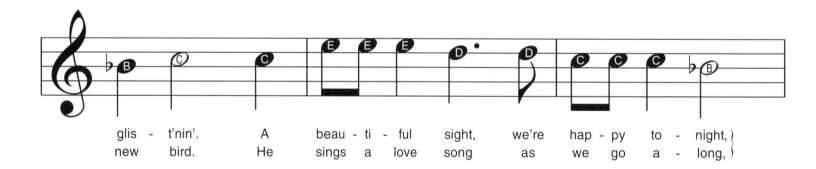

glis - t'nin'. A beau - ti - ful sight, we're hap - py to - night,
new bird. He sings a love song as we go a - long,

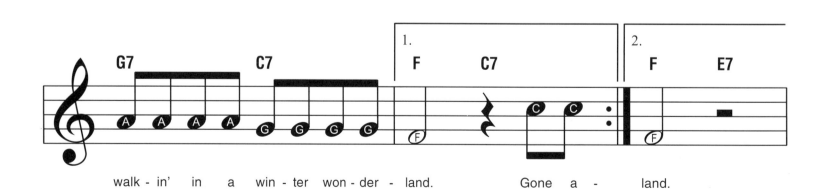

walk - in' in a win - ter won - der - land. Gone a - land.

You're All I Want for Christmas

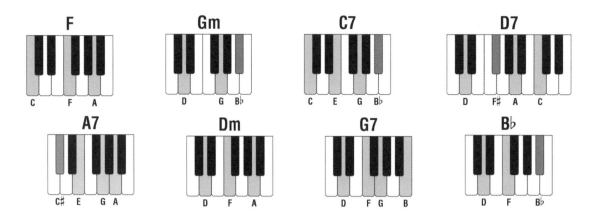

Words and Music by Glen Moore
and Seger Ellis

Moderately

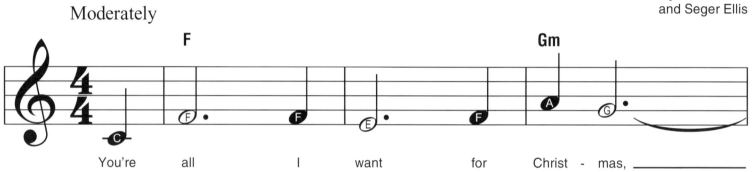

You're all I want for Christ - mas, _____

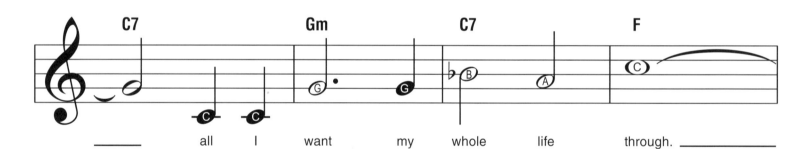

_____ all I want my whole life through. _____

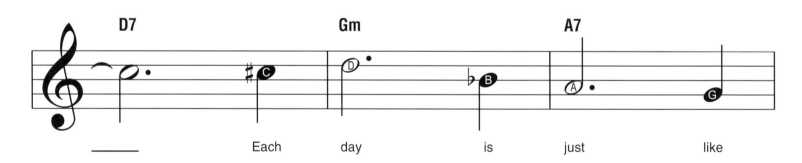

_____ Each day is just like

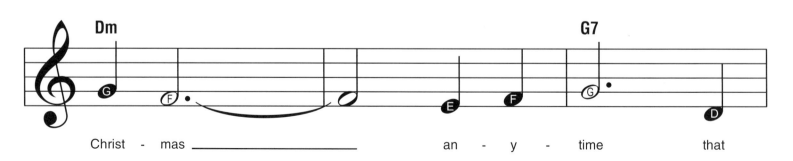

Christ - mas _____ an - y - time that

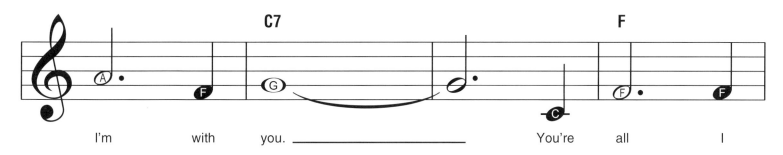

I'm with you. _____ You're all I

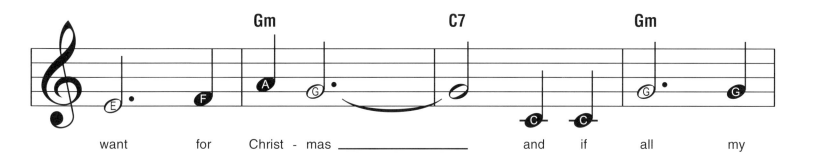

want for Christ - mas _____ and if all my

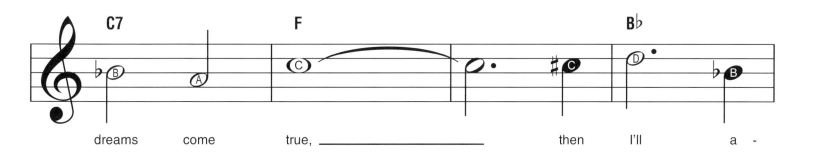

dreams come true, _____ then I'll a -

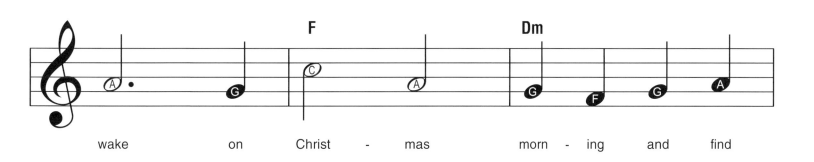

wake on Christ - mas morn - ing and find

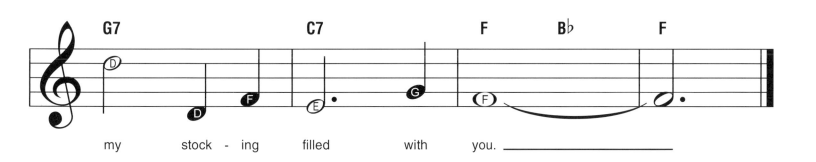

my stock - ing filled with you. _____

Wonderful Christmastime

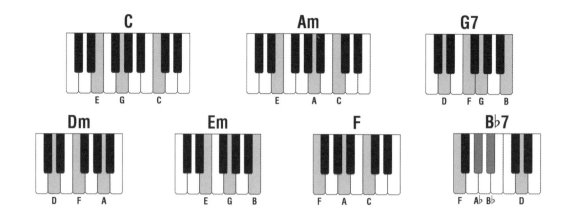

Words and Music by
Paul McCartney

Brightly

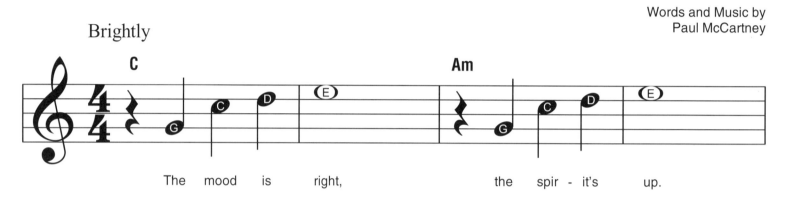

The mood is right, the spir - it's up.

We're here to - night and that's e - nough.

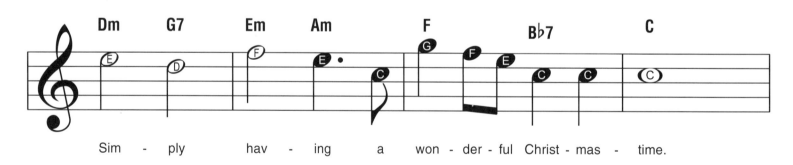

Sim - ply hav - ing a won - der - ful Christ - mas - time.

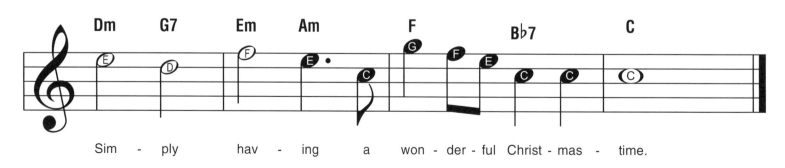

Sim - ply hav - ing a won - der - ful Christ - mas - time.